YOUR DAY, YOUR WAY

Inspirational Weddings

Jean Francis

Pen Press Publishers Ltd

First published in Great Britain by
Pen Press Publishers Ltd
25 Eastern PLace
Brighton
BN2 1GJ

ISBN 978-1-906206-10-9

Printed and bound in the UK

A catalogue record of this book is available from
the British Library

Illustrations by Karena Wiles
Cover design by Nick Webber

Dedication

To my son, Nick, his wife, Janette,
my daughter Carrie, and her husband, Brian,
who give me so much, ask for so little
and share my enthusiasm in all that I do.

About the Author

Until recently Jean Francis owned her own party planning and catering company, co-ordinating the many different occasions that mark life's milestones, such as birth, marriage and death.

This book offers practical advice with endless ideas to inspire the celebration of marriage and partnership ceremonies.

Jean has written this book following her life's involvement in creating special occasions, especially weddings.

Jean hopes that by purchasing this book you can halve the cost of your wedding.

Foreword

Weddings are always the happiest occasions. Everyone rejoices in the new union and the invitation to participate in the big day brings great anticipation. However, much planning and attention to detail precedes the perfect wedding day.

'Your Day, Your Way' will be of great value to the wedding planner. This book is divided into thirty-three easy to use chapters offering advice on a choice of wedding venues that include the traditional church setting, register office or spiritual ceremonies that can take place in a variety of locations, in woodland, in the garden, on the beach, in a barn, aboard a steamboat and on the moors. Suggested choices of flowers, music, reception venues and entertainment with a variety of transportation ideas from sleek limousines to a 1954 Dennis bus, complete with contact addresses are included in this valuable book. Weddings can be small and intimate or large and adventuresome; in fact, the choices are as wide as your imagination.

Jean Francis has drawn on her years of experience as a wedding planner and caterer to provide you with so many creative ideas to implement for your special day. Even if you haven't a wedding to plan, reading this book will provide hours of page-turning information that you could use for other celebrations.

Barbara Large

Author's Note

I cherish the memory of produce from Dad's vegetable garden, the first picking of new peas, tiny potatoes and scrambled eggs from our own hens. I suppose my passion for food, creativity and decoration is always at the heart of everything I do.

I grew up with a strong desire to have at least six children. I dreamt of making gigantic pots of hearty stew, enormous crusty pies and cakes using four dozen eggs like Mrs Beeton. Instead I married and had two children. I started a catering business and have continued to make gigantic amounts of food ever since.

Following an art school training I spent several years making and adorning costumes for the Royal Ballet and Opera at Covent Garden in London. I think my love of glitz originated there.

My work as a caterer began with making and icing my own wedding cake, shortly followed by christening and birthday cakes for Nick and Carrie. Orders came flooding in. Our kitchen soon became a hive of activity. I was joined by Christine, a lifelong friend also with two small children. Together we baked, iced and decorated between tending our children's needs.

Outside the infant school gates in the sixties I met Jenny, a professional and talented florist and mother of five. We decided to collaborate and pooled our ideas and skills, matching sugar flowers for the cakes with those in the bridal bouquets. We considered ourselves pioneers in this field. From wedding cakes and flowers a need became evident for a full catering service. We accepted the challenge, working from our homes, with our small children helping whenever they were able.

During thirty-six years of outside catering a wonderful network of helpers evolved, many are still best friends. We laughed and wept together on numerous occasions, but the good humour and laughter that refreshes the soul will never be forgotten. Without such special people this book could not have been imagined.

Now in retirement, using the experience of a lifetime I offer a service whereby using e-mail and telephone I can help plan the special occasions that celebrate the milestones of life. For details see the back of the book.

Acknowledgements

I would like to express my gratitude to all the couples who have allowed me to eavesdrop on their special moments and to everyone who, knowingly or unknowingly has contributed towards this book.

Thanks must be given to the catering team for their hard work, moral support, shared interest and recollections.

To the Revd. Lesley Edwards, the Revd. Jacqueline Clark and the Revd. Johanna Boeke for their inspirational contributions.

To Doreen Riches and Shivaun Hayes-Coles for creating order from the many scraps of paper and scribbled notes.

To Christine Johnson and Angela Gibson for being my devil's advocates and ruthless editors.

To Nick Webber for the cover photography.

To Karina Wiles for her artistic contributions.

My grateful thanks to the following people who have contributed to the book in different ways. Joan Sparrow, Angela Carroll, Ann Foley, Debbie Allum, Marie Schlotter, Penny Tryhorn and the Revd. David Richards.

To Barbara Large without whose help and encouragement I would never have taken the first step.

Finally to Pen Press for making it happen.

Introduction

A tin of bully beef inspired this book. An elderly friend spoke about her own wedding that took place during the Second World War. Her fiancé returned for an unexpected period of leave bearing a tin of bully beef. This treasure acted as a catalyst for their wedding. They now had a delicious filling for the sandwiches to be used at the reception. A simple wedding was hastily arranged.

Today weddings are very different and having catered for hundreds I realise that the essence of a memorable occasion is linked to using a theme. Once this has been established as a focus, arrangements fall easily into place. Celebrations can be flamboyant or modest. The cost need not dictate the ambience, style or joy of the day.

Your Day, Your Way offers alternative ideas and guidance for planning your special day. It contains thirty-three weddings, each illustrating an individual theme with a different focus, selected to meet family circumstances, finances, spiritual beliefs and sexual orientation. This book is packed with ideas to spark the imagination that can be used in their entirety, or on a mix and match basis. It demonstrates that unusual venues can be converted into something unique and that themes can complement a season, a dream, a hobby, a holiday, a favourite colour or a particular tradition.

Couples of every age, their family and friends will glean inspiration from the pages of this book which abounds with special touches that personalise a wedding day. Every aspect is covered. 'Your Day, Your Way' is not a book on wedding etiquette or marriage law.

Contents

Wedding Services and Ceremonies

Your choice of wedding should reflect your beliefs, personality and style, in an honest and harmonious way. There are many choices to consider when designing a ceremony unique to you. Follow your heart, have the wedding of your dreams. Remember, it's YOUR DAY. Celebrate it your way!

WHERE AND HOW

Register Office: Before the marriage can be arranged, it is necessary for the couple to give notice of their intention to marry in the district in which they each live. Other legal requirements will be discussed at this appointment. A civil ceremony is conducted by the Superintendent Registrar and the Registrar; it follows a standardised format although most offices permit the addition of non-religious readings, poetry and music.

Church: This follows the rites and ceremonies particular to each faith. The words used must include the questions and answers that meet legal requirements. It offers for believers an opportunity to celebrate the beginning of married life in a place blessed by spiritual tradition.

Approved Buildings: Most non-religious ceremonies can take place in any building registered by the local authority with the Superintendent Registrar and the Registrar in attendance. Venues can include hotels, country houses, castles and many other places. Facilities for the reception are often available together with accommodation.

New legislation, once it is passed, will allow for an even wider choice by registering the person who officiates instead of the building in which the wedding takes place. Advice can be obtained from any register office.

Abroad: Complete wedding/holiday packages are available from most travel agents. They take care of all arrangements including travel, hotel, cake, flowers and photographers. It is still necessary to register your intention to marry at the register offices that serve the district(s) in which you live.

Using a Celebrant: Choose a celebrant who will personalise the ceremony, introducing an interpretation of your chosen theme. A wide selection of resources are available from which to choose the most fitting words and symbols. You can discuss in detail all aspects of the wedding or blessing and your personal preferences. The use of a Celebrant alone does not legalise the marriage. A civil ceremony will also be necessary.

The Civil Partnership Bill: The Bill became law on 21st December 2005. From this date same sex couples can legalise their partnership within a civil ceremony that provides them with all the same rights as those of a heterosexual union.

To the best of the author's knowledge the information in this book is correct at the time of publishing. Nevertheless, always ensure that you check all legalities before making any arrangements.

Tying the Knot in an Ethical Way

There are enormous environmental and social impacts associated with weddings, so why not consider making your day 'green'? Adopting a considerate and thoughtful approach to planning your special day will create awareness in others and be acknowledged as a reflection of your personal values. An ethical wedding does not need to compromise on style. By adopting the right attitude we can all make a difference to our precious environment, preserving the privileges that we have enjoyed for future generations.

General information:
www.greenunion.co.uk
Ethical weddings:
www.ethicalweddings.com

Rings:
Search in antique shops for a unique engagement ring, or seek out gold that can be recycled into your own design and consider fair trade silver. If choosing new rings ensure that the diamonds are from a conflict free source.
www.stepheneinhorn.co.uk
www.greenkarat.com

Invitations:
Nothing could be more personal than making your own invitations. Use recycled-paper for the wedding stationery, or simply send the invitations via e-mail.
Wedding stationery:
www.thenaturalstore.co.uk

Hen and Stag Parties:
Choose local entertainment to avoid environmentally unfriendly long distance travel.

Bridal Wear and Flowers:
The 'something borrowed' could be your wedding dress. Alternatively search on-line or in charity shops for dresses, usually worn only once and often representing a huge financial saving. For the attendants, ensure that the outfits can be used afterwards for other occasions. Whether you buy, make, re-model or hire, use natural organic and fair trade fabrics wherever possible. Buy locally grown flowers avoiding hot house and out of season blooms that travel thousands of air miles.

Bridal-wear:
www.wholly-jo.co.uk
Shoes:
www.beyondskin.co.uk
Flowers:
www.utani-uk.com

Transport:
Try to arrange the wedding and reception within easy walking distance of one another and have a traditional wedding procession. For longer distances consider hiring a bus or coach to transport guests, or arrange for them to share rides. Avoid gas-guzzling limos, instead ride horse-back, travel in a horse drawn carriage or have a friend pedal you to your wedding in a bicycle rickshaw.

The Wedding:
Locate a venue that is registered for civil ceremonies where both the wedding and reception can take place under one roof. Throw biodegradable confetti, fresh flower petals or blow bubbles all of which are eco-friendly. Remember that dancing fountains and acres of manicured lawns have an environmental impact.
Natural confetti:
www.confettidirect.co.uk

Drinks:
Buy Fair Trade or locally produced organic wines and beers wherever possible. Use glassware or recycled disposables, avoiding plastic that does not bio-degrade. Make sure that all empty cans and bottles are recycled.
Wines:
www.festivalwines.co.uk

Refreshments:
Hire caterers or choose a venue that will accommodate your requests for locally grown organic food and support local suppliers. Use biodegradable tableware or china where possible, china-hire packages that include the washing up are available. To keep costs down organise a shared meal, asking guests to bring a dish of food and make the wedding cake using fair trade ingredients. Instead of decorating tables with cut flowers, use potted plants or a single bloom that guests can take home with them.
Biodegradable tableware:
www.ecoproducts.com

Departure:
There are many romantic honeymoon destinations that do not clock up air miles, consider travelling by sea or by train. When you fly your CO_2

emissions add to climate change, these can be offset by funding sustainable energy projects.

Climate Care:
www.climatecare.org

Gifts:
Choose ethical gifts, thus encouraging guests to support community projects in third world countries. If you enjoy gardening ask for trees, shrubs or garden vouchers, every plant planted helps to 'offset' and reduce an equivalent amount of harmful greenhouse gasses. Many couples already have all they need and a request for donations to be given to a charity is a thoughtful touch.

Gift ideas:
www.oxfamunwrapped.com
www.naturalcollection.com
www.ourgreenweddinglist.com

HARVEST MOON

*A harvest wedding was followed by a rustic reception
in an ancient barn for sixty guests.*

It was when my daughter married that I learned to listen.
Having lived in a catering environment all her life she obviously
felt threatened by the possibility of 'posh nosh'. Looking back
I appreciate and admire her simple but imaginative ideas. A combination of sophistication and rustic charm sprang together like
a dream. The occasion was able to accommodate a stepmother
and stepfather in a convivial way due to its sheer informality.

Action Plan:
Carrie and Brian decided to theme their wedding around their
deep love of the countryside. Being a keen horsewoman, Carrie
was familiar with all the quaint haunts within the neighbourhood.
Eighteen months before their intended wedding date they set about
a tour of discovery. Having located a suitable 17th century barn they
approached the farmer who gave his permission for it to be used
for their reception. During the week preceding the wedding a
frenzy of activity took place, with the removal of livestock and an
intense cleansing programme.

Brian and Carrie contacted the local vicar who advised them of
all the legal requirements necessary for their marriage.

When this wonderful wedding took place sixteen years ago, health
and safety regulations were not as restrictive as they are today.
Although catering was my business and it was a private function,
we proceeded to make the arrangements with due diligence and
care. Being in possession of employers' and public liability insurance was reassuring.

Invitations:
For a personal touch the invitations were handmade. Carrie organised
a bridesmaids' night in, when they made the
embossed invitations using a combination of
rubber-stamping and watercolour. The design
gave a hint of what was to come with a note:
"There will be barn dancing on an earthen

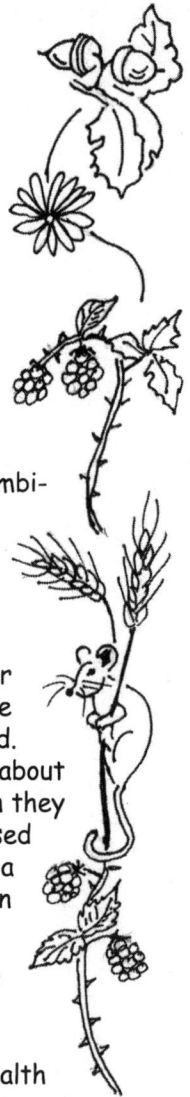

floor. Please bring suitable footwear.' The invitations were sent out three months prior to the big day.

Hen and Stag Parties:
Carrie, with a group of her girlfriends spent a luxurious few days at a health spa where between sessions in the Jacuzzi they were soaked, steamed and wrapped in seaweed, mud and honey.

Brian's male friends arranged a weekend of golf, playing at some of the more famous courses. They spent the evenings propping up the bars,

Bridal Wear:
Carol, my friend, designed and made both Carrie's and her bridesmaids' dresses. As she lived nearby, she gave them fittings at unearthly hours to accommodate their erratic work schedules. Carrie's dress was made in the palest pink wild silk. The idea for her train was inspired at a fitting in our sitting room that Hugo the florist attended to co-ordinate the floral requirements. Flourishing yards of net and grasping flowers from a vase he and Carol conjured up the perfect train, one that would follow Carrie up the aisle but being in two lengths could be draped over her shoulders in the barn. Both trails were finished with tiny silk bows and fresh pink rosebuds.

Hugo created her floral headdress and hand-tied bouquet, which continued the country theme and contained pink old English roses, combined with treasures from the hedgerows that included acorns, herbs and blackberries.

Groom's Wear:
Brian and his best man, Nick, wore identical morning suits in silver grey with matching top hats and waistcoats. They chose pink and grey striped cravats and wore pink rosebuds in their buttonholes.

Attendants:
The two bridesmaids Zoe and Heather wore dresses in gentle shades of purple and green shot silk. Their bouquets echoed the style of Carrie's but included highly scented purple roses.

Photography:
Steve the photographer and family friend, was with Carrie as she put the final touches to her make-up and when Hugo secured her beautiful floral headdress in place. Steve took 'fly on the wall' and formal photographs throughout the day, including the farewell firework display.

Marriage Ceremony:
The marriage took place in a medieval chapel, which by sheer good fortune

was decorated for Harvest Festival. The building was festooned with produce and brightly coloured flowers with sheaves of corn lining the aisle. The service followed the traditional Church of England celebration of marriage.

Transport:
When the formal photographs had been taken, the newlyweds were driven in style in a sensitively refurbished pony trap drawn by a single bay mare. Taking the short cut to the reception they made their way at a leisurely pace along the old drove road where autumn leaves were changing colour and berries glowed in the hedgerows. Guests in motor vehicles took the longer route via the main road.

The Setting:
The ancient wooden doors of the barn were open, not on this occasion for hay carts but to welcome the guests. Sunshine and warmth poured in, highlighting a tangle of autumn berries, leaves and michaelmas daisies in shades of pink and purple that cascaded from the hayracks. Natural greenery was plentiful, ivy had over the years forced its way through the many cracks and crevices in the old timbers. Circular tables clothed with gingham were set between the cattle stalls and straw bales covered with rugs provided seating.

Drinks:
As guests arrived they placed their gifts in an old milk float that stood in a corner of the barn. The contents of the parcels were a surprise as the couple chose not to mention presents in their invitations.

Guests were offered drinks while being welcomed by Carrie and Brian, a choice of country wines; damson, blackberry and redcurrant were among the selection on offer. The popular choice was a cocktail consisting of a dash of crème de muir, topped up with dry sparkling wine with the addition of a blackberry. Cattle troughs were filled with glistening ice where bottles of champagne awaited the toast. Meanwhile music drifted from the hayloft where the musicians played throughout the reception.

Refreshments:
The buffet was laden with a typical farmhouse spread of cottage loaves, English cheeses, pickles, relishes, homemade pies and pasties and wooden trugs full of prepared whole salad vegetables. Among the desserts were large dishes of blackberry and apple pie, greengage tart and bramble mousse. These were served with local ale, dry cider or wine. I prepared the meal and it was served by my team of helpers who ensured everything ran smoothly despite using a stable as a kitchen, with only an electric urn and hosepipe for water.

Cake and Speeches:

When the meal was finished, attention focused on the cutting of the wedding cake. Four tiers of iced basketwork were piled high with more treasures from the hedgerow spilling from between each tier. On the top tier sat a tiny mouse on a toadstool looking as though it had just crept out of the woodwork. This ornament provided Brian and Carrie with a treasured keepsake.

During the speeches the newly married couple toasted one another and their guests using champagne flutes engraved with ears of corn and their initials. These were a most appropriate and thoughtful gift to the couple from a close relative.

Carrie's brother Nick, conscientiously carried out his responsibilities as best man. During his speech he couldn't resist teasing his sister. Rarely seeing her in a dress he took a peek wondering whether she was wearing jodhpurs beneath her wedding gown.

Entertainment:

As formalities drew to a close the most senior and responsible of the family's golden retrievers gently carried baskets of flowers by the handle, one to Brian's mother and one to me. When the toasts and good wishes were complete the band played 'Congratulations' from the hayloft. This introduced barn dancing, which proved to be ideal entertainment as experience was not necessary and it suited all ages. Beginning with basic steps the dances were tailored to the ability of the dancers. The first dance was 'Lucky Seven'. The caller encouraged the men to form a large circle with ladies forming a circle on the inside. As the music began the ladies introduced themselves to their partners before moving on to the next. 'The Gay Gordons' followed.

Departure:

Having changed in a stable Brian and Carrie prepared to leave. Guests followed an old fertility rite of showering them with corn from an adjacent bin before they drove into the moonlight accompanied by a short display of colourful fireworks.

Gifts:

Throughout the reception a friend sketched the wedding scene that was eventually captured in oils and became her gift to Carrie and Brian.

Notes:

Mobile toilets were hired. See Yellow Pages.

No smoking signs were placed throughout the barn.

Alison, the hairdresser spent the morning at our house dressing hair, manicuring nails and helping in many other ways.

The bouquets and headdresses were hung in an airy, dark place to dry and still nestle dustily among the beams in Carrie and Brian's cottage. After the wedding Carrie and I made a garland using dried plant materials collected from the wedding, incorporating her veil, champagne corks and other small items of memorabilia.

EBONY AND IVORY

A register office marriage that was followed by a reception in a piano/cocktail bar for twenty-six guests and one dog.

Friends are made under many circumstances. Kevin and I met while walking our dogs. Realising that I worked as a caterer, he told me about his forthcoming marriage to African-born Tara, whom he had met while working on the local newspaper. In spite of being unable to cater for their wedding, we drank wine together one evening and exchanged ideas. It was from this meeting that the Ebony and Ivory theme developed.

Action Plan:
Kevin and Tara decided on a small, sophisticated yet informal occasion to celebrate their marriage. Having both been married before, they were anxious that just a few close friends should share their happiness. It was agreed that Digger, Kevin's impeccably behaved boxer dog, should be included in the celebrations.

When arranging the register office wedding Tara and Kevin were advised of the date by which the legal preliminaries should be completed. They were asked by the registrar to produce the relevant documents including their decrees absolute. As Africa is outside of the European Economic Area Tara had to produce one of the following:

- A current, valid passport showing an entry clearance specifically for the purpose of marriage in the UK.
- A 'Certificate of marriage approval' obtainable from the Home Office.
- A current, valid passport showing an 'indefinite leave to remain'.

Invitations:
The couple chose to have an evening cocktail reception. 'Black tie' invitations featured a piano keyboard and when the envelopes were opened a shower of music shaped confetti appeared, leaving no doubt as to the theme of the occasion.

An enclosed note read: 'As you are probably aware Tara has had breast cancer twice. We are of course very grateful for her wonderful recovery. We ask that rather than bringing gifts to our wedding, you consider making a donation to the Macmillan Cancer Relief Fund that does such a fantastic job nursing those less fortunate than Tara.'

Bridal Wear:
Tara's dress was close fitting and floor-length made in lined ivory georgette. The back featured a low bias draped neckline flowing elegantly into a small train. Her headdress was created from scarlet and black feathers. She wore a necklace of cowrie shells, which are found on the west coast of Africa. Once they were used as currency but, on this occasion, symbolized purification, beauty and power. Her bouquet of waxy scarlet anthuriums and lightly gilded greenery was beautiful but simplicity itself.

Groom's Wear:
Kevin wore a black necktie and white silk shirt with his dinner suit. Digger also attended the reception, impeccably accessorised in a black bow tie.

Civil Ceremony:
Having arrived by taxi, Tara and Kevin's on-line register office marriage took place using web-streaming technology so that members of Tara's family could watch the ceremony 'live' in Cape Town. Although religious music was not permitted, they chose songs of love. The couple made their vows to one another using words from the heart, exchanged matching platinum rings and signed the marriage register observed by friends from near and far.

Photography:
Informal, journalistic-style photography suited the couple's requirements and followed the black and white theme. A colleague captured a complete photographic record of the day, including a photograph of the clock in the registrar's office as Tara and Kevin made their commitment to one another. Following the ceremony, photographs were taken in an attractively paved garden behind the register office.

The Setting:
The reception was held in the piano bar of a hotel. Tall chrome stools surrounded the glass-topped bar with a few smaller tables and chairs available. The pianist played a selection of music, which included Gershwin and Porter jazz classics and songs from Broadway shows.

Floral arrangements were simple but dramatic. Scarlet anthuriums were arranged with clusters of shiny gold baubles, gilded palm leaves and spear grass.

Drinks:
The barman shook cocktails to order. Black Russian was the popular choice, a combination of vodka, coffee liqueur and ice. Sparkling blackcurrant was offered as one of the non-alcoholic alternatives.

Refreshments:
Selections of canapés provided an elegant reception and continued the black and white theme as follows:

- Sushi.
- Stuffed mushrooms.
- Tiny caviare boats.
- Miniature kebabs made with cherry tomatoes, cubes of feta cheese and black olives.
- Chequerboard sandwiches in brown and white bread.
- Smoked salmon on triangles of dark rye bread.
- Oysters.
- Strawberries dipped in dark chocolate.
- Tiny blackcurrant tarts.

Small black and white serviettes were fanned for both convenience and effect on each tray of food.

Cake and Speeches:
Champagne was poured from sophisticated matt black bottles for the toasts. The barman made a small slit in the first cork to be pulled. Into the incision he wedged a silver coin minted in the year of the couple's marriage, giving it to them as a keepsake.

Tara and Kevin cut their wedding cake, which was a collaboration of rich, dark and white chocolate, fresh raspberries and cream.

Kevin's speech was brief but humorous. In it he congratulated his wife and dog on their appearance, adding with a twinkle in his eye "that he hoped they would apportion his attentions in an agreeable way, because he didn't want to end up literally in the dog house." A friend proposed a toast to the couple and presented them with a copy of the Tara and Kevin Special Edition that had been printed by their colleagues. The contents were photographs from childhood, poems and anecdotes, which had been contributed from a variety of sources. Embarrassment was soon overcome by laughter.

Departure:
Before leaving, each guest was given a copy of the Tara and Kevin Special Edition as a souvenir. The newly married couple accompanied by Digger left by taxi. *En route,* they called at the local hospital where Tara delivered her bouquet and a copy of the Special Edition to a sick friend.

Gifts:
Instead of receiving gifts the couple sent a considerable donation to Macmillan Cancer Relief Fund. For details of different ways to donate Tel: 020 7840 4628 or 020 7840 4654

Notes:
If you do not have Kevin and Tara's contacts and would like your own special newspaper, contact Page One.
Website: www.pageoneexclusive.co.uk

ORANGES AND LEMONS

A late spring wedding for eighty guests was followed by a marquee reception in the garden of the bride's family home.

Following the initial excitement of their engagement, Lorraine and Sam felt overwhelmed, not knowing where and how to start making arrangements for their big day.

Action Plan:

The conservatory where we were sitting as we discussed ideas for their wedding was bursting with exotic blooms including orange and lemon blossom. The sweet-scented flowers, dark glossy leaves and fruit inspired us to adopt a citrus theme. Besides, orange blossom is a symbol of fertility!

Lorraine made an appointment for Sam and herself to meet the vicar of her parish church to make arrangements for their wedding. The couple also attended preparation sessions to discuss in detail the significance and commitment of marriage.

Invitations:

The invitations were decorated with golden bells giving the time, date and place of the wedding. Guests were asked to RSVP and to indicate any special dietary requirements on the enclosed reply card. An information sheet was also included giving the following information:

- Directions to the church and reception.
- Details of local accommodation.
- A request that no confetti be thrown, although rice was permitted at the church.
- A footnote suggested that for guests wishing to provide a gift, vouchers from a popular store would be appreciated to help buy items for the couple's new home.

Hen and Stag Parties:
Lorraine's married sister, Juliet, who was to be maid of honour, arranged a hen night for her sister and a group of friends. The party enjoyed a five-course meal on board an old steam train, which journeyed between stations.

Sam's best man organised the stag night. As the women tucked into their meal the men were aboard the real ale train where bar snacks could be ordered. Periodically the two trains passed on the track. When this occurred glasses and spirits were both raised.

Bridal Wear:
Lorraine's Regency-style dress was made in pale lemon silk voile over taffeta, with a pin-tucked bodice, short sleeves and a low-scooped neckline. On her head she wore a full wreath of orange blossom and carried a bouquet of calla lilies, scented freesia, yellow roses and orange blossom.

Groom's Wear:
Sam, his best man and the ushers wore traditional morning dress with tangerine brocade waistcoats and a sprig of orange blossom in their buttonholes. Lorraine purchased a pair of personalised socks for each male member of the wedding party, the wording on the socks described each of their roles for the day; groom, best man, usher, father of the bride and father of the groom.

Attendants:
The two five-year-old bridesmaids wore ballet shoes with their lemon ankle length dresses and wide tangerine sashes around the waist. Between them they carried a floral rope that matched the flowers in their hair.

Juliet, the maid of honour, chose a sleek, full-length gown in tangerine satin, she wore a floral headdress and carried a bouquet similar to that of the bride.

Transport:
Lorraine's father had for many years been re-furbishing a 1913 Clement Bayard. It had been Lorraine's dream to be driven to her wedding in the old car, 'Clemmie' as she was affectionately named. Following much effort on behalf of her father he finally pronounced the vehicle roadworthy when she passed her MOT! Lorraine's dream came true as her father drove her to church in Clemmie.

Photography:
The work of their chosen photographer had a contemporary look with a sense of movement. Natural, un-posed images combined with traditional portraits created an album that reflected the wedding day perfectly.

Marriage Ceremony:

An abundance of colourful and fragrant flowers filled the church; gerbera, broom, roses, bells of Ireland and mimosa, all of which followed the citrus colour scheme.

Ushers distributed the order of service sheets and showed guests to their seats. Traditionally the bride's family and friends sit on the left-hand side of the church and the groom's on the right.

Lorraine married at the parish church where she and her family regularly worshipped. With her father she made her entrance to 'All People Who On Earth Do Dwell' the Old Hundredth, sung by the choir.

Juliet took charge of her sister's bouquet during the actual marriage ceremony.

Handel's 'Where E're you Walk' was sung by a soloist as the newlyweds signed the marriage register.

For the couple's triumphant procession down the aisle at the end of the service 'The Waltz of the Flowers' was played as the church bells peeled joyfully.

The dainty floral pew-ends were removed discreetly after the service and used as table decorations for the reception.

The Setting:

The garden of the bride's home offered an ideal setting for the marquee. A red carpet laid beneath a covered way led guests through a floral archway where clusters of golden bells, flowers, ivy and long flowing gold ribbons formed a spectacular entrance. The marquee glowed with flower balls that hung from the ceiling containing a proliferation of orange, lemon and lime blooms with spiralling gold ting-ting and halved citrus fruits.

Drinks:

Guests were offered drinks on arrival, tall glasses of champagne or non-alcoholic St. Clements, a combination of orange juice and lemonade. More champagne flowed from a tabletop fountain from which people were invited to help themselves.

While the bride and groom received their guests, a selection of light canapés were served as three saxophonists wandered casually among the crowd playing in perfect harmony.

Refreshments:

Circular tables were formally laid with linen cloths in the palest shades of orange and lemon. Matching napkins folded and tied with gold ribbon lay on the side plates and the pew-ends became table arrangements. Guests checked the seating plans to find their seats. Miniature orange trees with a plant tag bearing the name of each guest decorated each place setting. Similar tables were prepared for the bridal party and elegant gold chairs completed the scene.

Bottles of red and white wine together with still and sparkling mineral water were placed on the tables and replenished regularly. The leisurely meal was served from a well-equipped service tent and consisted of:

- Spinach and carrot roulade.
- Granary rolls and butter.
- Medallions of pork cooked in a creamy citrus sauce with toasted pine nuts and garnished with kumquats.
- Courgettes stuffed with lentils and walnuts were provided for the vegetarians.
- A selection of fresh vegetables.

Cake and Speeches:
Instead of a traditional wedding cake, a two-tiered circular table festooned with fabric and flowers formed a centrepiece to the marquee. Chocolate and orange gateaux were displayed, that doubled as cake/dessert, one for each table. The saxophonists played 'When I Marry Sweet Lorraine' as the bride and groom together delivered a gateau to every table where plates, serving tools and jugs of cream had already been placed.

In his speech the father of the bride gave a humorous account of his efforts to prepare 'Clemmie' for his daughter's wedding. He ended with a request that everyone join him and his wife in a toast to the "Bride and Groom."

Sam responded by thanking both sets of parents for their love and support. He also thanked friends and family for coming along to help celebrate their special day and proposed a toast "To our beautiful Bridesmaids and Maid of Honour." He then handed over to Dave, his best man popping in a joke or two as he had a good idea of what was about to come, "I'm not going to stand here and make fun of my friend, life's too short – and so is Dave. His relatives are all the same. In fact his family tree is a stump."

Dave who was rather short in stature produced an orange box onto which he defiantly climbed to propose the toasts and make his reply. "Ladies and Gentlemen, first of all, I must say what a thrill it is to be making a speech in a room that could be Pavarotti's night-gown!"

He continued with some one liners:

"The last time I made a speech in a marquee, I was so funny I brought the tent down".

"I don't know whether you know but my uncle used to be in the tent business but it folded."

Before climbing down from his pedestal he mentioned that the individual orange trees were a gift to each guest as a memento of the day, and that coffee and petit fours were being served from a side table. This gave Sam and Lorraine an additional opportunity to circulate among their guests before leaving.

Departure:
Having decorated the going away car, the best man announced that the newlyweds would shortly be leaving for their honeymoon. Everyone gathered as the bridesmaid's floral rope now reinforced with wire was held high forming an archway under which Lorraine and Sam passed as the saxophonists played 'Oranges and Lemons say the Bells of St. Clements.' As Lorraine reached the door she looked back and threw her bouquet towards a group of friends. The girls all jostled to catch it because traditionally whoever succeeds is the next to marry. The newlyweds left in a shower of confetti with a 'Just Married' sign attached to the back of the car.

Notes:
The best man and groom had read 'Mitch Murray's One-liners for Weddings and How to Use them in Your Speech' published by Foulsham.

Personalised socks are available from: Forever Memories Ltd.
Tel. 01384 878111
Website: www.forevermemories.co.uk

The stag and hen nights took place on the Mid-Hants Railway, 'Watercress Line', The Railway Station, Alresford, Hampshire. SO24 9JG.
Tel: 01962 733810

The champagne fountain was hired from Theme Traders:
Tel: 020 8452 8518
Website: www.themetraders.com

We extended our services to provide a cocktail party in the marquee at lunchtime next day to which guests staying locally, friends, neighbours and colleagues were invited.

WOODLAND WAY

A woodland wedding to which seventy adults and seventy children were invited with camping for the weekend as an option.

Having decided to write this book, a friend suggested that I talk to Lizzy and Andrzej. She knew that they had planned their special day with much thought, care and love. I spent a most enjoyable evening with the couple and their two daughters, re-living the event through a video and listening to stories of their day that reflected the nightmares, joys and hard work involved in organising such an occasion.

Action Plan:
Lizzy had been previously married. Polish born Andrzej and she planned a very personal and meaningful celebration with a Polish flavour that was to include Lizzy's two daughters, Emily and Claudia, family, friends and a large number of children. The couple made an appointment at the register office in their district of residence, to give notice of intention to marry. As Poland comes within the European Economic Area Andrzej needed only the standard documents.

Invitations:
Designed on their computer and using recycled paper, the text of the invitations was printed over a misty woodland scene. Guests were invited to camp for the weekend, book bed and breakfast locally or come for the day. The programme for the weekend mentioned that a hot meal would be provided for everyone after the ceremony.

Civil Ceremony:
Andrzej and Lizzy married quietly at a register office during the week. Their rings, which had been personally designed and made for them were kept to exchange during the woodland ceremony. The 'year rings' were engraved with the date of their wedding carved in Roman Numerals.

Hen and Stag Parties:

On the eve of the wedding, Lizzy and her friends relaxed for a while with glasses of wine after settling the excited children into their sleeping bags.

Andrzej spent his last night of freedom with the men sitting around a campfire exchanging stories and drinking 'tequila slammers'.

Bridal Wear:

Lizzy's dress was a shimmering combination of green, turquoise, pink and mauve that was created by using three layers of chiffon over shot silk. It had a handkerchief hemline and chiffon sleeves. She wore a coronet of fern and woodland flowers on her head and carried a matching posy that included a sprig of myrtle as a symbol of good luck.

Groom's Wear:

With his dark trousers and matching open neck shirt Andrzej wore a tapestry waistcoat that echoed the colours of Lizzy's dress.

Photography:

A friend produced a video and many others took photographs of the celebrations throughout the day.

The Setting:

Sixty acres of private woodland were hired for the weekend. The site offered basic toilet and kitchen facilities with some shelter. Guests who chose the camping option began to arrive on Friday evening.

Saturday morning dawned dry and warm, A friend of Lizzy's delegated tasks to willing helpers:

- Arranging flowers.
- Organizing the heating and service of food.
- Rehearsal of the circle dancing.
- The creation of a floral archway.

An old tree stump cascading with pink and purple blooms formed a centrepiece for the ceremony together with lighted candles and incense. A small silk cushion bearing the wedding rings had been placed on a nearby log.

Marriage Ceremony:

The band began to play a traditional Polish folk tune as the women and girls gathered to dance in the dappled shade, forming a circle around the decorated tree stump. Meanwhile the procession of men and boys could be heard drumming their way through the woodland, they interrupted the dancing by joining and enlarging the circle.

Lizzy and Andrzej wrote and conducted their own marriage ceremony.

They decided not to have an officiant but to enact the ceremony as a play. Several friends who took part were aware of the programme, ensuring that everything ran smoothly.

- Lynn Amanda introduced the proceedings.
- Claire read 'The Invitation' by Oriah Mountain Dreamer.
- Andrzej spoke about his meeting with Lizzy, the love that developed and his pleasure at gaining two beautiful daughters.
- Claudia announced that her sister Emily would sing a Polish folk song called 'Hearts are not Servants' and gave a translation of the words.
- Emily sang accompanied by a guitar.
- Lizzy spoke about her joy at meeting Andrzej and getting to know and love him.

Standing beneath the floral arch the bride and groom shared with the assembled company their heartfelt feelings for each other. Emily carried the silk cushion bearing the rings to the couple as they made their vows.

Before leaving the circle Lizzy and Andrzej followed a pagan tradition. Holding hands they jumped over a broomstick symbolizing 'out of the old life and into the new.' Claudia and Emily scattered rose petals and the band played as guests drank wine in celebration of the occasion.

Refreshments:
Lizzy and her friends had spent several weekends cooking and filling the freezer with hearty casseroles. Guests sat either at picnic tables or on rugs to enjoy the feast that concluded with fruits of the forest gateau and ice cream.

Cake and Speeches:
Andrzej and Lizzy decided against having a wedding cake although they had at one stage contemplated serving a gigantic steamed syrup pudding with custard. Guests drank the couple's health in champagne before a few short speeches of thanks and congratulations were made.

Entertainment:
As dusk fell, strings of tiny lanterns glowed in the trees adding a touch of magic to the woodland. Numerous citronella candles were lit to deter the midges and similar unwelcome nightlife. A folk band played for dancing and revelries continued until late into the evening.

Departure:
Finally Andrzej led Lizzy into the woods where an igloo tent lined with luxurious rugs and decorated with flowers awaited them, which is where they spent their wedding night.

Gifts:
An ornamental ceramic plaque hand-crafted by a friend was one of the couple's favourite gifts. It bore their names and the date of the wedding.

Notes:
Lizzy had thoughtfully provided plenty of fresh bread and packs of instant soup to be available to everyone throughout the weekend.

In the hire agreement the woodland had to be left as found so everyone rolled up their sleeves to help. Andrzej and Lizzy were among the last to leave.

EAST MEETS WEST

A civil ceremony in a hotel for twenty-five close family members was followed by an Interfaith celebration and reception for one hundred and twenty guests.

I met Ajith and Emma at a friend's birthday party where they told me about their forthcoming marriage. I was able to introduce them to an Interfaith Minister who helped them design a ceremony drawing on the truth and beauty of both cultures.

Action Plan:
British born Ajith often met Emma by chance in their local Indian takeaway. This led to sharing meals and eventually a proposal of marriage.

Their developing friendship was far removed from the traditionally arranged marriages of Ajith's family culture. The couple wished to respect and combine some of the traditions of both countries within their wedding celebration. Ajith took Emma to consult an astrologer regarding the most suitable date. They also had their horoscopes read. After a long search they found a hotel where the reception could be held that also had a registered marriage room.

Ajith and Emma made an appointment with the registrar in their districts of residence to give notice of their intention to marry. They each took along a valid passport or birth certificate and proof of address.

Invitations:
Written both in English and Hindi the invitations were made in India and decorated with mirrored sequins and embroidery. The envelope included a map of the area showing the nearest railway station together with an accommodation list.

Instead of wedding presents the couple requested vouchers towards their honeymoon and included details of the travel agent concerned.

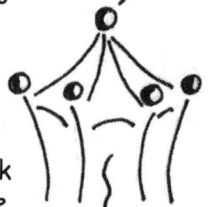

Transport:
The white saloon in which Emma travelled to her wedding was randomly dotted with tiny sprays of fresh red rosebuds and fern. She had seen and admired such a bridal car on a recent visit to India.

Bridal Wear:
Emma wore an ankle-length loose-fitting dress of western design, which was made in rich, red Indian silk, the colour worn by Indian brides. Gold silk ribbons were attached to one shoulder of her dress to be used in the marriage ceremony. Following tradition, Ajith's family would have given his bride saris and jewellery as a wedding gift; instead they paid for Emma's dress to be made and she accepted with pleasure the beautiful gold jewellery, which she wore for her wedding.

A friend painstakingly decorated Emma's arms and feet in a delicate pattern using henna, cunningly concealing Ajith's initials within the design.

Groom's Wear:
Ajith and his brother, Amish, who was best man both wore Western style suits. Ajith wore a garland of fresh flower heads that was given to him by his mother, which is an Indian tradition.

Civil Ceremony:
A civil marriage took place in the registered marriage room in the hotel and was witnessed by the couple's immediate family and conducted by the Superintendent Registrar and her colleague. The couple made a declaration of their freedom to marry before exchanging vows. At the conclusion of the ceremony the newlyweds signed the register along with two witnesses, thus completing the formalities.

The Setting:
Notes from a flute filled the air as additional guests received a traditional Indian welcome by having a garland of brightly coloured flower heads placed around their necks. A statue of Lord Ganesha the elephant-faced Hindu God of good fortune created a spectacular centrepiece. He was surrounded by a collage of purple, orange and golden blooms. Thick white candles and musky perfumes offered a promise of the east. Emma had hoped to include fresh exotic flowers in the arrangements but due to expense, silk blooms were hired and supplemented with every-day flowers and gilded greenery, achieving the desired effect.

Marriage Ceremony:
Everyone gathered in the hotel garden where a four-pole canopy, garlanded with flowers had been erected. The couple removed their shoes before the celebrant introduced herself and welcomed everyone to the marriage of Emma and Ajith.

The blessings of the Gods were invoked by the celebrant as Emma offered yoghurt and honey to Ajith as a token of purity and sweetness. Ajith recited a Vedic hymn to Kama, the God of love, for pure love and blessings. Facing one another with hands on each other's hearts the couple made the vows they had written. A flautist played as Ajith placed a ring set with Indian rubies on the third finger of Emma's left hand. The minister then wrapped the gold ribbons attached to the bride's dress around the shoulders of the groom symbolising their sacred union. To show that Emma was now a married woman her husband carried out a tradition from North East India by putting red powder in her hair. Having removed the garland given to him by his mother, the bride and groom garlanded one another with fresh flowers. They walked seven times around the nuptial fire together and made seven promises before being showered with rose petals.

When the ceremony had ended the couple went to replace their shoes but Ajith's were missing. Following Hindu tradition the bride's sister had hidden them. He was only allowed to have them back in exchange for money.

Photography:
It was important to the couple that the photographs were creative because many would be sent to Ajith's relations and friends in India who had been unable to attend the wedding.

Drinks:
Sparkling wine, ice-cold Kingfisher beer and a selection of exotic fruit juices were provided, together with traditional Indian yoghurt based Lassi.

Refreshments:
The celebration buffet was a combination of food from both countries. An extensive selection of vegetarian curries; hot and spicy, sweet and sour, dry and aromatic and some very, very hot were served with accompaniments together with traditional British fare. Dessert was a choice of English apple pie and fresh fruit salad.

Cake and Speeches:
Glasses of sparkling wine or fruit juice were distributed in readiness for the toasts.

Ajith began his speech by telling his new wife how beautiful she looked. He went on to tell the story of how he and Emma had met and how they spent a wonderful holiday in India where Emma collected many ideas for the wedding.

Amish read out messages from friends who were unable to be with them on this special day. Toasts being a British tradition, everybody was anxious to join in and many far away places and people were mentioned.

Amish eventually gained the attention of the crowd asking that everybody raise their glasses to the bride and groom, wishing them health, wealth and happiness.

Before the cake-cutting ceremony took place, he spoke about an old English custom, whereby girls used to put a slice of wedding cake under their pillow for three nights to dream of the man they would marry. This idea caused a great deal of amusement, especially among the Indian ladies present.

The red and gold theme was carried through from Emma's dress to the cake, which consisted of two heart shaped tiers of dark fruitcake that were covered in rich red sugar-paste and decorated with fine gold piping.

Entertainment:
A tapestry of music and dance followed. The music was a fusion of Indian sitar and tablas woven creatively with guitar and voice. The singer, a western girl, was dressed in a shimmering pink and gold sari. Her voice alternated between heartfelt English lyrics and Sanskrit chants. She ended her entertainment with a traditional Katak dance, the bells around her ankles tinkling in time with the vibrant and complex rhythms of the music.

Departure:
Before leaving, Emma and Ajith were again garlanded with fresh flowers and showered with petals to wish them good luck in their new life together. Emma's sister gave the bride a silver horseshoe as a typically British token of good luck.

Before the newlyweds' car departed, a coconut was placed beneath the front wheel and everybody waited for it to be broken by the weight of the vehicle. The custom originated when horse drawn carriages were used in order to ensure that the wheels were roadworthy for the journey. (Traditionally, this procedure would have taken place on the vehicle that transported the groom to his wedding.)

Notes:
The Interfaith ceremony was written and conducted by
Revd. Jacqueline Clark. Contact The Interfaith Seminary.
E-mail: admin@theinterfaithseminary.com
Website: www.theinterfaithseminary.com

For musical entertainment and Indian dance workshops contact Garima.
E-mail: Garima@utlworld.com

The sprays of fresh rosebuds and fern were attached to the wedding car with Blu-tac.

For astrological consultations and readings contact Robert Alan Haven.
E-mail: robertalanhaven@onetel.com

HIGHLAND FLING

*A Burns' Night Supper for sixty guests was preceded by
a secret Gretna marriage and Scottish honeymoon.*

Trying to arrange a traditional wedding with such complicated family circumstances became a nightmare to Anna and Derry. They worried about who would give the bride away, who would sit in which position in church, receiving lines and table plans. Finally they decided to follow in the footsteps of Anna's grandparents who eloped to what used to be known as Gretna Green, to be married under local law.

Action Plan:
To celebrate this special occasion they decided to invite family and friends to join them for a Burns' Night supper on their return from Gretna at which their secret marriage could be divulged.

Anna and Derry sent to Gretna for an information pack, enclosing an A4 stamped, addressed envelope. Arrangements were made for the marriage according to Scottish law. The couple were also required to give notice of their intention to marry in the districts in which they had lived for the seven days prior to their marriage.

Derry and Anna travelled to Scotland just in time to celebrate the New Year, which was followed by their romantic Gretna marriage and a skiing honeymoon.

Invitations:
The invitations doubled as Christmas cards and invited relatives and friends to a Burns' Night Supper with Scottish dancing. Guests were requested to 'dress with a Highland flavour, the funnier the better.' Derry and Anna hoped that by introducing humour a light-hearted atmosphere could be achieved.

Bridal Wear:
For her wedding Anna wore a long white velvet dress, her voluminous cloak in dark green was trimmed with white swans' down and not only looked incredibly glamorous but offered

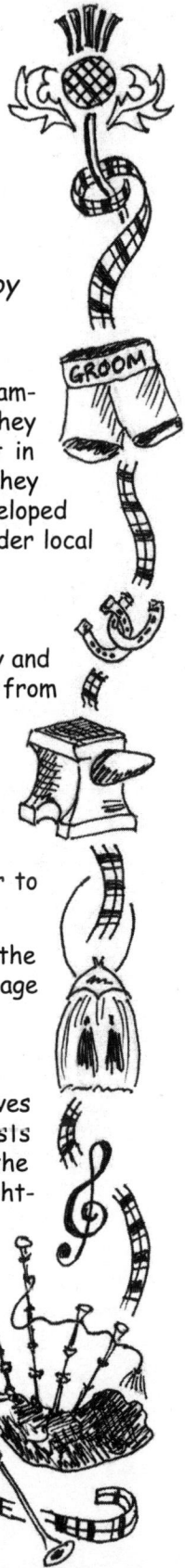

GRETNA GREEN

comforting warmth. On her fur muff was pinned a sprig of white heather tied with tartan ribbon.

Groom's Wear:
Derry wore a lounge suit for the wedding with a white shirt, tartan tie and a sprig of heather in his buttonhole.

For the party Anna wore her wedding dress with the addition of a Braveheart tartan sash, worn diagonally across one shoulder and secured by a brooch.

Derry hired full Scottish dress; a double-breasted jacket, wing collar shirt and bow tie that he wore with a Braveheart tartan kilt, decorative sporran, jabot and skean-dhu tucked into his white hose. Beneath his kilt he wore a pair of boxer shorts on which the word 'Groom' was printed thus identifying his role.

Photography:
Table cameras were provided for guests to photograph anything that took their fancy. These were collected at the end of the evening and the film later developed. Derry's boxer shorts caused much laughter and became well documented on film.

Drinks:
In the splendour of their Highland dress the newly married couple mingled with their guests. Among the alcoholic tipples offered was a hot whisky punch or a 'wee dram' together with plenty of alternatives. Scottish smoked salmon canapés were handed round as the 'skirl' of bagpipes provided an authentic flavour to the gathering.

The Setting:
It was a cold January. The village hall they had chosen proved to be the ideal venue, warm, with good kitchen, toilet and car parking facilities and a polished floor that was perfect for dancing. The hall was large enough to allow for the supper to be held at one end and dancing at the other. An additional smaller carpeted room was available where aperitifs were served and guests could sit quietly to chat.

White linen cloths with tartan overlays were laid on long tables with a miniature bottle of whisky in each place setting. The piper, followed by Derry and Anna arm in arm, led everyone around the hall to supper. When the music stopped, guests were asked to take the nearest chair, this idea resolved any need for table plans. When they were all settled, the piper proceeded to pipe in the steaming hot haggis, which was carried traditionally on an ornamental platter by the chef in his whites. After the compulsory 'wee dram' of whisky and using his well rehearsed accent Derry recited Robert Burns' 'Address to the Haggis' which began:

'Fair fa' your honest, sonsie face,
Great Chieftain o' the Puddin'-race!
Aboon them a' ye tak your place,
Painch, tripe or thairm:
Weel are ye wordy o' a grace
As lang's my arm.'

Refreshments:
Prepared and served by the caterers, starter portions of piping hot haggis, neaps and tatties were delivered to each guest. Everyone then helped themselves from the buffet that was laden with cold roast beef, Scottish salmon, hot potatoes and salads in abundance. Raspberries with whisky ice cream and shortbreads were served and followed with a selection of cheeses and oatcakes. Coffee was available from the buffet throughout the evening.

Cake and Speeches:
Derry and Anna's wedding cake was a traditionally iced whisky cake, decorated with silver horseshoes, sprigs of white heather and tartan ribbons. The cake cutting was followed by Derry's short and amusing speech when he formally announced their marriage that was no longer a secret. Toasts and congratulation followed.

Entertainment:
Dancing to a Ceilidh Band began. The caller's light-hearted humour provoked plenty of hilarity. The more mistakes that were made, the more everyone laughed. While dancers rested for a while, a comic demonstration of the sword dance and Highland fling created further amusement. As the evening drew to a close Derry hoped he had avoided the old Scottish custom whereby the groom's feet are washed in preparation for the couple to set out on their new path together. Some of his more high-spirited friends had earlier threatened to carry out this ritual!

Departure:
Derry wrapped his wife in her cloak as they stood at the door to bid their guests farewell before leaving themselves by taxi. Several of Derry's friends stayed behind to help clear the hall that had to be vacated by midnight and left clean and tidy.

Gifts:
Knowing Anna and Derry's passion for board games, they received a number including some cheeky ones.

Notes:
For an information pack enclose an SAE to: Gretna Registration Office, Central Avenue, Gretna, Scotland. DG16 5AQ.

Tel: 01461 337648
E-mail: gretnaonline@dumgal.gov.uk
Website: www.gretnaonline.net

Identifying boxer shorts and disposable cameras are obtainable from.
Website: www.perfectweddingstore.co.uk

PARALLEL LINES

A civil partnership celebration between two men was followed by a Humanist ceremony, with dinner and a casino evening on board a retired steamer.

The venue chosen for this party was a retired passenger and cargo steamer that could be hired out for functions. Having catered here before I remembered the difficulties we encountered manoeuvring heavy equipment on board, negotiating gangplanks, ladders and narrow stairways that resembled an obstacle course.

Action Plan:
Having met on holiday in Italy, Tony and Neville chose an Italian theme for their party. They wished to celebrate their partnership with dignity, while making a public affirmation of their love and commitment to one another.

The Civil Partnership Bill became law on 5th December 2005 and from this date same sex couples are able to legalise their partnership within a civil ceremony. This Bill gives them the same property and inheritance rights as married couples and other advantages in pensions, immigration and tax matters. Following legal requirements, The couple gave notice to the local authority in which they resided. The information given went into the public domain for the following fifteen days before their Civil Partnership could take place.

Tony and Neville, having no particular religious beliefs, planned a humanist ceremony to follow the register office formalities. This was planned with the help of a Celebrant and personalised in as many ways as possible.

Invitations:
Both men were artistically inclined, the invitations were therefore imaginative. Designed using a computer package the printed words were ironed on to a length of fabric.

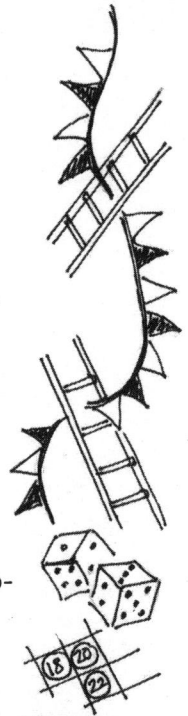

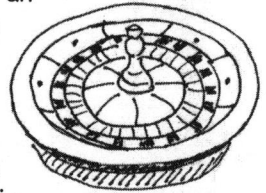

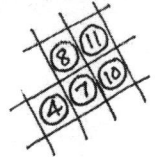

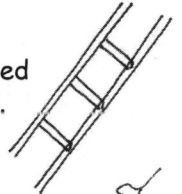

Guests were invited to the register office and afterwards the humanist ceremony that would be followed by dinner and a casino evening on board the SS Stargazer. The date, times and addresses were given with maps of both locations together with a note saying that instead of traditional gifts they would prefer guests to bring plenty of cash to spend in the casino, as the evening's proceeds would be donated to a local children's hospice.

Transport:
To add an extra special touch to their day the couple hired a silver stretched limousine, which was decorated with red and green ribbons.

Dress:
Neville and Tony dressed identically, in black trousers, gold lame jackets and black T-shirts decorated with golden starbursts.
Their sisters who acted as best women also dressed in black and gold to harmonise with their brothers.

Civil Ceremony:
A crowd of friends and family heralded the couple's stylish arrival at the register office. Tony and Neville tied the legal knot in a short ceremony. The legalities involved signing by the couple, two witnesses and the Superintendent Registrar of a partnership schedule.

The Setting:
On board SS Stargazer red and green bunting and balloons decorated the upper deck confirming the Italian theme. Tony and Neville posed beneath an archway of balloons for photographs as the musicians, two violins and a cello, played a selection of music chosen by the couple that created an atmosphere of celebration.

The catering team offered champagne and orange juice or a combination of both making Bucks Fizz. Guests drank to the future happiness of the newly bonded couple from tall glasses that twinkled with coloured lights.

Commitment Ceremony:
Everyone gathered excitedly on deck where chairs had been placed either side creating an aisle. Neville and Tony approached, one from each side and walked together to where the celebrant and best women waited. The celebrant welcomed everybody on board and explained the procedure for a Humanist ceremony, pointing out that throughout history rituals have been used to mark important events in people's lives. He spoke about Tony and Neville's civil partnership ceremony and read as follows:

The peace of the running water to you.
The peace of the flowing air to you.
The peace of the quiet earth to you.
The peace of the shining stars to you.
And the love and care of us all to you.

Both mothers were asked to step forward and join their sons. Neville and Tony had learned by heart the solemn promises they now made to one another witnessed by all those present. The best women handed the rings to the celebrant who blessed them before they were exchanged, both were engraved with the date and a personal message. After some selected readings the Celebrant offered his congratulations to the couple. To the strains of Madonna's 'Crazy for You' Tony and Neville signed a decorative certificate and everyone present added their signatures.

Drinks:
Having taken a dress cue from the theme, the catering team were dressed in straw boaters with patriotic hatbands, black trousers and white T-shirts. They served champagne and a selection of hot miniature pizzas topped with mozzarella cheese, tomato and basil.

Refreshments:
The long table was formally laid in the main saloon and decorated with low containers of red roses that had been sprinkled lightly with gold dust. Made by Tony, the crackers were crafted from red and green linen napkins each containing a small but appropriate gift, they also doubled as markers for the place settings. Red, green and gold sugared almonds were scattered on the table for decoration and to be eaten with coffee.

Served from the cramped galley the meal consisted of the following:

- Mushroom risotto.
- Beef in a rich red wine sauce
- Polenta.
- A medley of fresh seasonal vegetables.
- The meal was accompanied by a generous amount of Italian Chianti.

Cake and Speeches:
A tall stack of meringues and cream studded with red roses was served with a coulis of red summer fruits and doubled as a celebration cake.

Champagne continued to flow as the relaxed couple toasted their guests and one another. Speeches were made by both best women who in turn offered fond reminiscences of their brothers and read aloud several amusing mock telegrams. The speeches ended with an announcement that the bar was open and that drinks, including coffee and sambucca would be available throughout the evening.

Entertainment:
Friend Tom who had taken responsibility for organising the casino evening was dressed in a black tie and dinner jacket, in order to give a professional tone as casino manager. Other friends took part acting as cashier and croupiers. A dummy run had taken place earlier in the day ensuring that the casino volunteers were fully aware of the parts they had to play.

Everyone moved to the far end of the saloon where the cashier handed out instruction cards, changed real money into fun money and casino chips used to play the tables. Guests were able to purchase more fun money throughout the evening as required. The croupiers were available to teach guests the rules of roulette and blackjack if necessary.

The punter with the most money at the end of the evening won a Jeroboam of champagne that had been donated by Tom as a prize.

The recipient of the champagne raised yet more cash for the worthy cause by auctioning it off.

Departure:
Neville and Tony had planned a spectacular and noisy firework display to mark the finale of their wonderful day but cancelled the idea when they realised that firework regulations prohibit the use of fireworks at night between 11pm – 7am. As the couple crossed the gangplank to reach their getaway car they were bombarded with sweets, this being yet another Italian custom.

Gifts:
Substantial proceeds from the evening were donated to a local children's hospice.

Notes:
The British Humanist Association.
Tel: 020 7079 3580
E-mail: info@humanism.org.uk
Website: wwwhumanism.org.uk

The Pink Triangle Trust: 34 Spring Lane, Kenilworth, Warwickshire, CV8 2HB.
Tel: 01926 858450
E-mail: secretary@pinktriangle.org.uk
Website: www.pinktriangle.org.uk

To contact the Goyesca String Trio.
Tel: 0870 300 0984
Website: www.goyescastringtrio.co.uk

The Casino Fundraising package was supplied by Beneficial Arts.
Tel; 0870 735 3277
Fax:0870 735 3288

The computer programme used to make the invitations was
'Create a Print' using Avery software, code: C94055.

For flashing champagne glasses contact Glow Unlimited.
Tel: 01908 821175
Website: www.glowunlimited.com

Firework Regulations 2004 prohibit the use of fireworks at night between 11pm – 7am in England and Wales with extensions for certain public
festivals.

LAVENDER AND LACE

*A church wedding with forty-five guests
that was followed by a tea-dance.*

Corrine, her friends and I collected together our bone china,
dainty linens and cut glassware to add an air of luxury and individual-
ity to this special occasion.

Engagement:
Ray and Corrine shared a mutual fascination for antiques. At an auction they had purchased a box of miscellaneous pieces of china, some
of which matched Corrine's tea service. In the teapot was a ring of
considerable value, which despite being returned to the auction
house, remained unclaimed. Finding this beautiful ring became
the catalyst for their engagement.

Action Plan:
Both having been widowed, they wanted their special day to
be personal, unusual and memorable but they did not want to
spend a fortune. Their shared interest in antiques, together with
Corrine's discovery of an illustration of a 1930's outfit, confirmed
the theme for their wedding day.

Ray and Corrine discussed arrangements for their marriage with
the vicar, which included the calling of the banns.

Invitations:
Corrine made the invitations herself. Printed on handmade paper
with a lacy edge, the addition of a drop of lavender oil hinted at
the ambience of the occasion. The time, date and address of the
church and reception venue were clearly stated. Guests were
asked to indicate whether or not they wished to take advantage of
the special transport arrangements which were explained.

A note implied that the couple honestly did not wish to receive wedding presents but realised that tradition would prevail. A small
item towards one of their miniature china collections was
suggested, leaving friends to spend as much or as little as
they liked.

Bridal Wear:
The design for Corrine's dress was copied from an illustration of a 1930's day dress and was made for her in pale lilac silk by a dressmaker. The bloused bodice was low-waisted with an elegantly draped skirt. She wore grey accessories including a deep cloche hat for the church ceremony. Corrine was especially pleased when she found her shoes, which matched her dress exactly and had a T bar with diamanté and silver buckles.

She carried a tussy-mussy of English flowers; a tight posy of tea roses in faded antique pink, lavender heads, scented geraniums and herbs, encircled in a dainty lace frill.

Groom's Wear:
Ray, his son Tim who was best man and Ray's four-year-old grandson all wore lounge suits with matching waistcoats. Ray wore the pair of antique cuff links that were a present from his bride.

Attendants:
Corrine's twin granddaughters appeared to have stepped straight out of a 'Cries of London' scene. Wearing tightly laced black bodices over cream ankle length dresses they carried baskets full of deep purple lavender blooms.

Transport:
As suggested in the invitation, most guests parked in the town hall car park. Ray's passion for old vehicles led him to hire a 1954 Dennis bus, which transported the wedding party to the church in the heart of town and afterwards to the reception. Billowing with balloons and ribbons it was well in keeping with the occasion.

Marriage Ceremony:
The marriage ceremony took place at the parish church in which Corrine regularly worshipped.

She arrived on time, despite the tradition of the bride being late, and was escorted by her brother. The vicar waited at the entrance with the brides-maids to welcome her as the choir sang 'I was Glad' by Parry with organ accompaniment. As Corrine took her place beside Ray the vicar began with a greeting. The service was taken from the old Book of Common Prayer, using the beautiful language so familiar to many members of the congrega-tion. Corrine promised with a smile to obey Ray. Following the exchange of rings the couple were invited to kiss. While the newlyweds signed the marriage register a soloist sang 'Jesu Joy of Man's Desiring' by Bach.

The wedding party and their guests left the church as the choir sang the joyous and uplifting introduction to 'Zadok the Priest' by Handel.

By the time they reached the west door cameras were in full action. Tiny bags printed with their names and the wedding date were distributed by the bridesmaids and were full of biodegradable rose-petal and lavender confetti that was used to full effect, offering wonderful photo opportunities.

The wedding party climbed aboard the old bus for the return journey to the town hall.

Photography:
The wedding was captured in a fast, relaxed 'reportage' style giving a true feel of the day. Within the package Corrine and Ray included a few sepia shots, one of which was printed on canvas to hang in their home.

The Setting:
From a list of places for hire issued by the local council Corrine and Ray identified the Town Hall as being an ideal venue for their reception. Guests entered the building through the opulent red-carpeted foyer. To the left was a room with heavy oak panelling, stained glass windows and a polished floor that was ideal for dancing. To the right was a galleried room with crystal chandeliers. Here individual tables were laid for afternoon tea with delicate lace cloths and napkins, each with a bone china tea set of a different design. A bowl of fragrant roses, sweet peas and lavender on each table created a beautiful centrepiece.

Drinks:
After much persuasion one of the drinks team agreed to dress and play the part of an old-fashioned butler. He poured and offered a choice of sherries in antique glasses of varying designs from a silver tray. The jazz trio consisting of sax, keyboard and double bass played such classics as 'Jeepers Creepers' and 'Putting on the Glitz.'

Refreshments:
Waitresses, dressed as Lyons Corner House girls known in the thirties as 'nippies' wore black skirts with white aprons, cuffs and caps served afternoon tea. Each table formed its own individual party enjoying steaming pots of Indian or Earl Grey tea, plates of tiny cucumber sandwiches, asparagus rolls, scones and a selection of dainty iced cakes displayed on lace doilies. Home-made lavender ice cream was served to end the meal.

Cake and Speeches:
Handmade sugar flowers decorated all three tiers of the round cake. The two lower tiers were bonded together bearing tall pillars that supported the third. This was topped with a beautiful china figurine from Corrine's collection. A good quality sparkling wine instead of champagne was poured for the toasts and served in tall glasses. In his touching but amusing speech

Ray thanked the guests for sharing this special day before the best man proposed 'a toast to the newlyweds'.

Entertainment:
As the musicians played for dancing, Ray and Corinne gave a well-rehearsed Charleston display. When the applause had abated guests were encouraged to join.

Departure:
The couple left for their honeymoon with Ray driving his 1935 Riley Nine Special.

Gifts:
Most gifts were, as requested, small china pieces.

A collection of lavender bushes for their garden was a thoughtful and appreciated present.

Notes:
Vintage bus hire, Memory Lane:
Tel: 01628 825050
Website: www.memorylane.co.uk

Biodegradable rose petal and lavender confetti in personalised bags is available from:
Website: www.confetti.co.uk

Washing so many cherished items of china and glassware belonging to other people made me grateful that I was fully insured to cover the cost of any possible breakages.

Corrine's many personal and special touches that did not cost a fortune made the occasion so very memorable.

At the end of the party Corrine distributed the table flowers to family and friends.

TAKE TWO

*A double wedding celebration for fifty in late October
with one hundred additional guests joining the party
to dine, dance, breakfast and brunch.*

Having helped Rachael and Martin plan their wedding I was
shocked when Rachael telephoned to tell me that they had
decided to postpone the day due to the sudden death of her
father. Her disappointment was compounded by the fact that
her cousin and best friend, Sally, planned to marry later that year.

As the two families were so closely related, everyone seemed to be
connected. I sowed a seed of thought by suggesting they share a Dad
to give them both away and celebrate a double wedding. This idea
was considered and developed into a truly wonderful occasion.

Action Plan:
The majority of people would have attended both weddings. By
combining their guest lists the financial advantage enabled a
wedding day to become a weekend. Most importantly, Rachael
and her mother would be fully supported throughout.

The country club where Sally and Justin's wedding was already
booked, confirmed its availability and willingness to accommodate a
second wedding, offering exclusive use of the hotel for the weekend
with a flexible range of choices that could be tailored to the double
occasion. The final arrangements resulted in a combination of ideas
that were welcomed by both families. Using a well-recommended
toastmaster would introduce some formality to the occasion, ensuring that the programme ran to time. This arrangement would
relieve the bridal parties of social and emotional burdens.

Written quotations were obtained from all the providers concerned
and decisions were made as to how the costs would be apportioned.

Arrangements for the double wedding were discussed with the
Superintendent Registrar of the district in which the venue was
situated. It was confirmed that both couples must give
notice of their intention to marry in the districts in
which they lived, or have lived for the preceding
seven days.

Invitations:
The guest list was agreed by both families and invitations sent to close relations and best friends inviting them to attend the late afternoon civil marriage ceremony dressed ready for the evening. Black tie invitations were extended to a further one hundred guests who were invited to the champagne reception followed by dinner, dancing and a light snack at midnight. A champagne brunch next morning was also arranged, after which the newlyweds would take their leave. Guests were asked to indicate if they wished to order a vegetarian meal.

An accommodation tariff and a list of local bed and breakfast establishments were also enclosed.

Hen and Stag Parties:
Both young couples decided to spend an evening together with a group of friends at a nightclub rather than have separate parties.

Bridal Wear:
Each bride dressed individually. Sally wore a flame coloured chiffon dress with narrow shoulder straps and a slim fitting floor-length skirt and carried a bouquet of cream orchids.

Rachael's choice was a silver grey satin dress with a gently draped neckline, twisted straps and a floor-length skirt. Her flowers consisted of shell pink roses, mauve freesia and stephanotis.

Groom's Wear:
Martin, Justin and their best men wore dinner suits with black ties plus the addition of a flower in their buttonholes, matching those in their respective bride's bouquet.

Photographs:
A videographer was hired to capture the occasion and include random interviews, with a record of childhood shots being added later which especially pleased Rachael as many of these included her father.

Marriage Ceremony:
On behalf of the wedding party the toastmaster liaised between the registrar, videographer and venue manager, keeping the event running smoothly in spite of the tight schedule. He welcomed the wedding guests, showing them into a drawing room where champagne was served as they awaited the arrival of the bridal parties. Empty glasses were collected before guests entered the marriage room as no alcohol is allowed where a wedding takes place. Chairs for fifty guests had been arranged and members of all four families sat together. Sally's father appeared with a beautiful bride on each arm, he kissed the hand of both young women before retiring to his

seat. The ceremony included non-religious songs, poems and prose. After the exchanging of rings and signing the register, the newlyweds followed by their families and guests moved through into the reception hall.

Drinks:
Champagne cocktails and a selection of canapés were being served as additional guests joined the party. A chamber ensemble played both classical and popular pieces while a close-up magician mingled with the guests, performing card and magic tricks.

The Setting:
Much of the character of the country club resembled a stately home presenting an interior of elegance and comfort, with atmospheric lighting and fresh flowers.

The toastmaster called attention to the seating plan as everyone adjourned to the dining hall. The tables were laid with crisp white linen and enhanced further with tall decorative candelabra. Linen napkins were rolled and tied with ribbon with a single flower tucked into each one. Rachael and Sally had spent much time writing the menu and place cards in neat italic script.

A special candle of remembrance was set beside Rachael's mother that bore a photograph of her husband and was inscribed with the words 'always in our hearts'. After lighting the candle the toastmaster proceeded to say a Grace, which included the names of those unable to be present.

Refreshments and Speeches:
The meal was interspersed with toasts and speeches that were guided by the toastmaster who also requested that the gentlemen change places between courses taking their glasses and napkins with them.

The menu consisted of the following:

- Caesar salad.
- Beef Wellington.
- Sweet potato pie (for the vegetarians).
- Both main courses were served with a selection of seasonal vegetables.

When the time came for dessert, waiting staff processed in theatrical style around the room holding Baked Alaskas high above their heads. The mountainous peaks of warm meringue with a hidden core of ice cream were sludded with lighted sparklers. Desserts were taken, one to each table and served to the guests. This imaginative ceremony replaced any need for formal wedding cakes.

A full bar was available throughout the evening and guests were invited to order whatever they liked to drink.

Entertainment:

Following dinner and the last speech, everybody gathered on the balcony to watch a firework display, As a grand finale the sky was illuminated with messages of congratulations in fireworks to both couples.

The scent of flowers and flickering candlelight created a romantic atmosphere as a five-piece band began to play in the great hall. The toastmaster invited the newly married couples to dance the first dance. Justin and Martin set an informal tone to the evening by removing their jackets before leading their new wives onto the dance floor, changing partners for the second number. During the interval Martin, who had been a member of the band that had re-grouped for the occasion, played with them for a while. Finally the players sang a song for Rachael, Martin, Sally and Justin that they had written especially, resulting in much laughter.

Breakfast:

Following the last dance, well after midnight, a nightcap before bedtime was accompanied by a choice of omelettes or pancakes that were cooked to order with a wide variety of fillings.

All those who had booked to stay at the country club staggered up the elegant stairway, including the newlyweds, who were on their way to the recently renovated bridal suites complete with luxury four poster beds and double showers.

Champagne Brunch:

A mid-morning champagne brunch was served before the happy couples left for their individual honeymoon destinations.

Gifts:

A carrier collected both brides' bouquets during the evening while still fresh so that their beauty could be captured in ice using special techniques, before being photographed, mounted and framed. These keepsakes were a present from a family friend.
Tel :01344 291455

E-mail: debbiehare@btinternet.com

Notes:

Remembrance candles with photograph and inscription
Tel: 020 8521 5321
E-mail: info@remembrancecandles.com
Website:www.remembrancecandles.com

Jean Francis: 'Mentor of Milestone Celebrations'
Tel: 01403 273754
E-mail: milestone-celebrations@uwclub.net

EARLY BIRDS

A synchronistic meeting and a leap year proposal led to an early morning civil marriage ceremony followed by brunch for twenty-five guests.

Pete and Kathy met in a pub while selecting a record on the jukebox. The moment their fingers touched the same button and their eyes met, was the moment they fell in love. The record they chose was 'Leader of the Pack' by the Shang-ri-las, revealing them both to be, guess what? Motor-cycle crazy!

Action Plan:
After getting to know one another, Kathy took advantage of it being a leap year to propose to Pete, the one day in one thousand, four hundred and sixty one, when traditionally a woman can propose to a man. Pete accepted. Together they arranged an informal celebration, which included their offspring from previous marriages and a few close friends.

When they visited the registrar's office to give notice of their forthcoming marriage, both Kathy and Pete were required to take with them the following documents:

- A valid passport or birth certificate.
- Proof of address.
- Decree absolute.

Invitations:
The invitations were obtained by mail order. Kathy sent head and shoulder shots of Pete and herself to the artist. A realistic caricature resulted, with them both dressed in wedding attire on Pete's treasured Harley Davidson. The invitations came with a choice of coloured envelopes and inserts for the message. Their change of address card was also enclosed.

Hen and Stag Parties:
For her hen party, friends took Kathy first to a cocktail bar and then on to a lingerie shop. Here she was encouraged to try on the underwear of her choice.

The catch was that she was expected to parade the chosen items, which she did, bringing out her talents as an actress. Friends then bought the favourite pieces for her as a wedding gift. The fashion parade was followed by dinner.

Pete's male friends took him on a paint-balling experience. Wearing bunny ears and a fluffy tail over his overalls Pete became an irresistible target. After no time at all he was covered from head to toe in a spectrum of coloured paint, which would normally mean it was down to him to buy the drinks! But this evening he was treated to a pub meal and plenty of beer.

Bridal Wear:
Kathy wore a classic style trouser suit in mulberry linen with a cream, wide brimmed hat. In keeping with tradition, she wore something old, something new, something borrowed and something blue, which was an ornate beribboned garter. She carried a bunch of cream tulips, which included hoops of gilded and beaded spear grass.

Groom's Wear:
Pete and his brother, Gerry, who was best man, wore lounge suits with cream shirts and mulberry silk ties with matching handkerchiefs tucked into their top pockets.

Photography:
To save expense the couple decided not to bother with formal photographs, knowing that there would be plenty of digital images to admire and enjoy at a later date.

Marriage Ceremony:
An early appointment was booked at the register office allowing adequate time for the reception and their long honeymoon journey. Rings of intricate artistry were exchanged during the civil ceremony, which was witnessed by their children and friends. The party walked across the park towards the pub where they had first met and where their wedding breakfast awaited them, pausing only for a few photographs.

The Setting:
A log fire provided a warm and fragrant welcome in the bar where background music played on the radio and highly polished tables were laid ready with bottles of tomato and brown sauce.

Drinks:
Bucks Fizz was served with tomato and tropical fruit juices as alternatives. For those who preferred something longer and stronger, the bar was open. On the radio a request was played for the couple relaying a message of congratulations from Kathy's colleagues, the request was for the couple's special song, 'Leader of the Pack'.

Refreshments:
Gerry gathered everyone's attention and then said grace, "God, please bless this bunch as they munch brunch." The mouth-watering aroma of grilled bacon drew everyone's attention to the food. Guests helped themselves from the buffet, tucking into sausages, bacon, mushrooms, black pudding, tomatoes and eggs, which were cooked to order by the chef. Waffles with maple syrup, croissants, preserves and plenty of hot coffee were also on the menu. Mulberry coloured serviettes printed with the names of the bride and groom and the date of the wedding provided a personal touch.

Cake and Speeches:
Following the hearty meal, tall, slim glasses of chilled champagne were served. Gerry asked everyone to raise their glasses as he proposed a toast to the newlyweds. His toast was, "Long life and happiness."

Using one-liners his speech was punctuated by uncontrollable peals of laughter as he continued:

"I don't know if you heard but Kathy proposed to Pete on her hands and knees. She had to, he was under the table at the time."

"I think this is such a good idea, getting married early in the morning. That way, if it doesn't work out you haven't wasted a whole day."

"Today isn't like breakfast at home, you know. There they fix breakfast together, he makes the toast and she scrapes it."

And later, "The place they are going to for their honeymoon I understand, is so far off the beaten track that even crows don't fly there".

"But I tell you the surest way to save a marriage from divorce is not to show up at the wedding in the first place."

"Finally this is just a word to Kathy, husbands are like old kerosene lamps, they are not particularly bright, they smoke all day and they go out at night."

When the laughter had abated, Pete replied thanking Gerry for his predictable humour, which was exactly why he was asked to take on the role of best man. The bride and groom toasted one another and their guests.

Kathy felt a traditional wedding cake would be out of place for this particular occasion. Instead, she ordered a tiered cake stand on which small cone-shaped boxes containing chocolate dragees, tied with mulberry coloured ribbon were arranged, every guest received one to take home. Before leaving, just for old time's sake, Pete and Kathy played a few old favourites on the jukebox.

Departure:
Having substituted her elegant hat for a helmet, Kathy changed into leathers before departing on Pete's beloved and treasured Harley Davidson. He

kick-started the engine and it sprang to life. They both felt exhilarated by the smell of oil and hot metal. Kathy climbed aboard behind her husband with her un-crushable bare essentials in a pannier bag, still clutching her bouquet. They moved away to cheers of good luck, congratulations and a trail of old tin cans. Looking back, Kathy threw the bouquet towards her friends. Traditionally, the girl who catches it is supposed to be the next to be married.

The youngsters made their way back into the pub towards the entrance to the skittle alley.

Gifts:
The couple's children clubbed together to buy a set of limited edition prints by the well known artist, Roy Barrett, all featuring motorcycles from a past era.
Tel: 0130 886 2430
Website: www.art-of-motoring.co.uk

Notes:
Wedding invitations from Olde'n Ugly.
Tel: 023 8020 7759.
Website: www.olde-n-ugly.co.uk

Personalised serviettes available in different colours and cone shaped boxes containing chocolate dragees can be ordered from Celebrations.
Tel: 0845 130 8181
E-mail: sales@weddingrealm.com
Website: www.weddingrealm.com

Gerry's jokes were taken from 'One-liners for Weddings and How to Use Them in your Speech' by Mitch Murray published by Foulsham.

FRENCH CONNECTION

*A Catholic ceremony of marriage
followed by a French style reception on the Sussex
Downs for forty guests.*

Tom's mother and I liaised regarding the catering and detailed arrangements for the weekend celebrations. These involved hotel bookings, hiring loos and transporting furniture between the village hall and the downs. With only the van as a base from which to serve the wedding breakfast, a simple menu was required, which turned out to be the key to success.

Proposal:
Tom invited Anna Marie for a lunch date requesting that she bring her passport. They flew to Paris for a romantic day of sightseeing where he popped the question at the top of the Eiffel Tower.

Action Plan:
French-born Anna Marie and Tom agreed that they would risk the weather when planning their long lingering French style lunch on the Sussex Downs. The village hall was booked just in case of rain, which enabled us to use (by arrangement) the trestle tables and chairs. These were transported to the chosen site early on the morning of the wedding, which thankfully dawned bright and sunny.

Anna Marie had been brought up in the Catholic faith and wished to marry in the church where she worshipped although Tom was not a Catholic. The priest helped with their choice of hymns and readings, e-mails were exchanged until every detail was agreed.

Partly due to the fact that her father was not in good health, Anna Marie chose not to be 'given away' during the marriage ceremony.

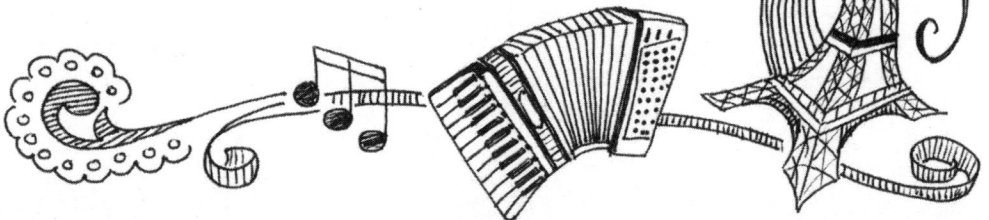

Invitations:
A simple but stylish impression was given by the handmade invitations that were written in both French and English and decorated with a sketch of the Eiffel Tower embracing Big Ben. The invitation gave the date, time and place of the wedding and reception. An enclosure detailed travel arrangements, a list of local accommodation, a programme of weekend activities and a date by which replies were required. It was also suggested that guests wear suitable clothing and footwear for an outdoor reception.

The couple's wedding gift list was included, providing them with an opportunity to expand their collection of glass, cutlery and tableware.

Bridal Wear:
Anna Marie's wedding dress, both traditional and elegant, was made in ivory silk with a soft textured sheen. On her head she wore a small spray of white marguerites that held her veil in place. She carried an armful of the same flowers that had been picked from a field earlier that morning, together with a handkerchief edged with delicate lace made by her grandmother.

Groom's Wear:
Tom and his best man wore morning dress with a single marguerite in their buttonholes.

Transport:
The flags of both countries were flying and the couple's names on the front plate, as the red London bus collected guests from their hotels. On the way it stopped to pick up the groom and his best man, who, to everyone's amusement, were thumbing a lift on the roadside. Put at the disposal of wedding guests for the weekend, the hired bus offered an opportunity for car drivers to have a relaxed break with no parking or drink driving worries. The jolly crowd was already gathered at the church gates to welcome the bride as she arrived with her parents in a taxicab.

Marriage Ceremony:
The church was decorated simply with terracotta pots full of white marguerites that lined the aisle.

The priest greeted the couple at the church door. Holding hands they walked behind him towards the altar steps followed by family and friends who found seats, as the organ played the 'Hallelujah Chorus' from Handel's 'Messiah'. The bride and groom made their vows to one another both in French and English, repeating a few words at a time after the priest. As the couple were joined in matrimony the rings were blessed and sprinkled with holy water. They agreed to bring up any children under the 'Law of Christ and his Church'. The organist played 'Air on a G String' by Bach during the signing of the register. As the newlyweds made their way down the aisle, their path was strewn with laurel leaves thus following an old French custom.

Photography:
Biodegradable confetti was thrown over the new Mr. and Mrs. as they posed for photographs that were creative and natural with a sense of fun. Tom's colleague, using his digital camera, took informal shots. These were later downloaded on to a computer and transferred to a CD ROM and e-mailed to friends near and far.

The Setting:
Tom and Anna Marie joined their guests on the bus for the journey to the country. On arrival it parked close to a sheltered ridge in the downs, just a short walk from where long tables were laid ready with checked cloths and decorated with terracotta jugs full of white marguerites. Views of the undulating countryside and farmland with distant glimpses of the sea were visible from where everybody gathered.

Drinks:
From beneath a canvas awning, fine French wines and pastis were served with olives of every imaginable variety. Glasses were raised to toast the newlyweds. The word 'salute' merged with laughter and music that was played on an accordion by a dapper Frenchman wearing a beret and stripy T-shirt.

Refreshments:
The food was displayed like still life arrangements on handcarts presenting a memorable and visual delight to diners, each course being of traditional French country fare. The meal began with a selection of savoury tarts and continental meats with enormous bowls of dressed salad and freshly baked baguettes. Anna Marie's relatives brought with them from France an impressive array of cheeses from many regions, to be eaten with figs and other small fruits. The many choices of mouth-watering desserts included Tom's favourite pot au chocolat.

For the service of this meal 'the team' dressed in snappy striped T-shirts and berets.

Cake and Speeches:
Tom and Anna Marie chose a croquenbouche; a traditional French wedding confection made up of cream-filled profiteroles, piled high, studded with flowers and beribboned with trails of spun sugar. Friends stood in a circle around them as they served the first portion. Toasts were made in both languages as the couple drank traditionally from a two-handled cup that belonged to Anna Marie's family and had been passed down for several generations.

In his speech the best man, who was Tom's school friend, recalled a number of amusing stories about their shared adventures as boys.

The accordionist played 'Under the Bridges of Paris' in true Parisian style as the newlyweds took the opportunity to mingle with their guests.

Departure:
Anna Marie and Tom left in a taxi that had been called by mobile telephone (having checked the previous day that there was a signal). Meanwhile the bus stood by ready to transport the guests to their respective destinations.

Further Entertainment:
A typical English fish and chip supper was provided for everyone later that evening, with Anna Marie and Tom joining the party for a short while. A guided sightseeing tour of the city for those who wished to take part was arranged for the next day prior to guests departing on their homeward journeys.

Gifts:
Anna Marie's mother observed an old French custom with her choice of gift for the couple. Following the birth of her daughter, a tree had been felled that had later been crafted into a chest. Prior to the wedding the couple's names and the date of their marriage had been carved into the lid. The chest contained an invaluable collection of household items amassed over many years.

Notes:
Following a custom from Belgium, the handkerchief carried by the bride on her wedding day was framed and kept until the next family wedding.

RIVER CRUISE

A celebratory Thames river cruise and reception for seven that followed a civil marriage ceremony.

We discussed the wedding arrangements over coffee, sitting on the riverbank outside Ann and Charlie's beautiful Mill Cottage. I felt it a great privilege when Ann, a long-standing friend, asked me to do the catering for their wedding day cruise.

Action Plan:

Charlie's contract was to take him to foreign parts for three years. He and Ann decided to tie the knot before leaving. This left little time to sell their home, ship the contents abroad, plan a wedding and honeymoon. They would have liked to have invited everyone, but with so many good friends and two families it was extremely difficult to know where to draw the line without offending any-body. Finally they decided to ask two friends who acted as wit-nesses, Ann's daughter and Charlie's two teenage children, who formed the party of seven.

Ann and Charlie gave notice of their intention to marry in the district in which they had lived for the preceding seven days. This notice was displayed on the Superintendent Registrar's notice board for fifteen clear days before the certificate could be issued for their marriage. The notice stated where they wished to marry.

The small group drove from the country to a hotel in London where they all spent the night before the wedding.

Invitations:

Due to the circumstances, invitations were given and arrangements made by telephone with the few people concerned.

JUST MARRIED

Bridal Wear:
Ann chose an elegant cream trouser suit in lined georgette with which she wore a pearl necklace and matching earrings. She carried a tight, hand tied, posy of peach rose buds.

Groom's Wear:
Charlie wore a dark grey suit with a carefully chosen silk tie, to tone with the flowers in Ann's posy.

Civil Ceremony:
Their civil marriage took place at Chelsea Register Office conducted by the Superintendent Registrar and the Registrar. It included the statutory words in which the couple made a declaration of their freedom to marry and exchanged vows and rings. At the conclusion of the ceremony, Ann and Charlie signed the register witnessed by their children, two witnesses and the registrars. The marriage certificate was presented, thus completing the formalities.

The Setting:
Following the ceremony the bridal party took a leisurely stroll along the embankment in the warm autumn sunshine. I walked to meet them with a tray of glasses and a bottle of chilled Champagne. Drinks were sipped while viewing the shimmering river scene set out before us, before making our way down to the jetty where the dazzling, white cruiser bobbed gently on its mooring.

The luxury vessel was billowing with balloons and ribbons with a discreet 'Just Married' banner attached to the stern that became an invitation for much horn blowing and jollity from other river users. As the wedding party embarked, a CD selection of light wedding music was playing.

Photography:
The photographer who had accompanied the bridal party throughout the marriage ceremony and for their walk along the embankment took more photographs on the cruiser before leaving.

Drinks:
As the vessel eased away from its mooring champagne and soft drinks with canapés were served on the upper deck.

Refreshments:
White linen napkins encircled by rings of variegated ivy decorated the table in the saloon where the lunch was set out and consisted of:

- Melon boats with Parma ham sails.
- Glazed and decorated fresh river trout.

- Hot new potatoes in parsley butter.
- Fresh asparagus.
- Green beans.
- Tossed mixed salad.

Puddings were served on the upper deck. Unfortunately the meringues blew away and the wind caught the glass bowls full of red fruits. Everybody and everything was covered in red spots, pudding was not a success! I have wished many times since that I had suggested my popular champagne jelly, in which, if set quickly, the bubbles become encapsulated. Served with the addition of cubes of mango, passion fruit and topped with decorative cape-gooseberries, the result would have been a delicious pudding with no mess!

Entertainment:
The cruise continued with the ever-changing landscape and vistas of the city passing by. During his commentary the skipper told numerous anecdotes as he pointed out the many sights of interest along the waterfront. We cruised past the imposing architecture of the Palace of Westminster, St. Paul's Cathedral and the Tower of London and beneath the many famous bridges including Tower Bridge. As the vessel approached the Thames Barrier the skipper accelerated to full speed, creating a fine misty spray before making a U-turn for the return trip.

Cake and Speeches:
A small rich fruit cake iced and topped with a cluster of sugar rose buds, matching those in Ann's posy was cut in the snug cabin, where toasts and a few short speeches were made. Ann and Charlie gave each of their children and their two friends significant and beautifully wrapped gifts.

As the cruise drew to an end, coffee and handmade chocolates were served.

Departure:
The vessel moored alongside the jetty in readiness for passengers to disembark. As the newlyweds stepped ashore, they found themselves surrounded by cascades of tiny bubbles blown by the younger family members.

Notes:
The CDs of wedding music were borrowed from a library.

PAST TIMES

A civil marriage that was followed next day by a medieval banquet for sixty guests and included a homage ceremony.

Tracy and Tim dreamed of having a party with a difference to celebrate their marriage. This theatrical theme transported me back to my employment at The Royal Opera House in Covent Garden, making costumes for the opera and ballet many years ago.

Action Plan:
Being keen members of an amateur dramatic society, the idea of a medieval banquet appealed to them. With much excitement they began to plan this flamboyant occasion. By adopting such a flexible theme the arrangements fell easily into place. The couple discovered a Tudor Merchants' Hall that was listed by their local council as being available for public hire. At first sight they fell in love with this beautiful old building that offered the perfect setting for their party. Before making the final booking Tracy and Tim went to view the interior when it was prepared for a function, checking that the lighting, heating and general space met with their requirements. Authentic tableware was hired, together with costumes for the serving staff and props to decorate the venue.

A date was set and arrangements made in good time for the civil marriage ceremony, to take place the day before their party.

Hen and Stag Parties:
A week before the wedding, wearing her 'Bride To Be' badge. Tracy and her friends spent a fun filled evening 'on the town' at a Revue Bar, moving on afterwards to a disco.

For his final fling as a single man, Tim was whisked away by a group of his friends for a surprise weekend of beer and archery.

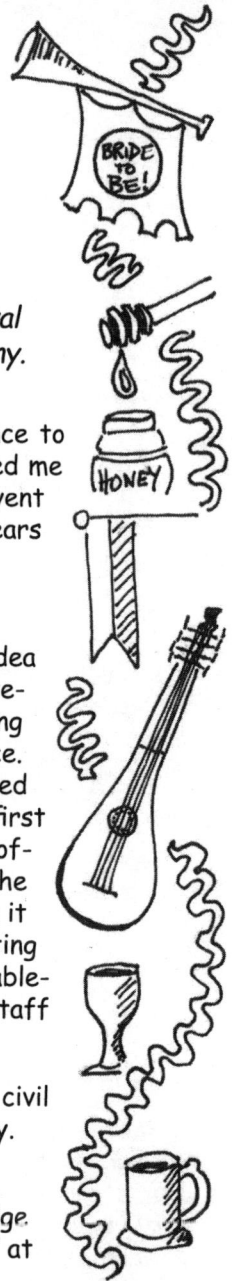

Invitations:
A parchment scroll sealed with wax and tied with red ribbon invited guests to celebrate the marriage of Lady Tracy and Lord Timothy with a homage ceremony, that would be followed by a fine banquet with music, cavorting and dancing till late. Guests were requested to dress in medieval costume. A map with directions was enclosed together with the wedding gift list that was lodged at a local department store.

Civil Ceremony:
Tim and Tracy received their marriage certificate following a short civil ceremony at the register office conducted by the Superintendent Registrar and Registrar with two close friends as witnesses. The couple did not exchange rings, preferring to save this moment to be a part of the ceremony next day.

Bridal Wear:
Tracy wore a circlet of flowers on her long dark hair. Her dress was made of midnight blue velvet with a laced bodice decorated with intricate gold embroidery.

Groom's Wear:
Tim wore a long tabard style tunic with coloured woollen hose and his best man who acted as Burghermaster dressed in a similar way.

Transport:
Tracy had always been a keen horsewoman but before the wedding she took lessons in riding side-saddle. She and Tim rode in costume through the town to their celebration party. As they approached, guests ran into the cobbled courtyard to greet and welcome the bridal pair.

A local stable accepted responsibility for collecting the horses.

Photography:
A unique photo opportunity presented itself as Tim and Tracy arrived in style and dismounted. They posed against the historic building that offered a perfect backdrop for the photographs. Disposable cameras were distributed, enabling guests to capture every cherished moment on film.

The Setting:
The impressive Tudor Merchant Hall, with its whitewashed plaster set between blackened oak timbers had an air of grandeur. Passing beneath the low arch, flanked by tall octagonal towers, the party moved inside.

Drinks:
A flight of stone steps led upwards onto the city wall where 'wenches' served mead and ale from earthenware jugs. Guests viewed the pano-

ramic views as minstrels played, using a selection of medieval instruments including a lute, crumhorn, sackbut and recorder.

Homage Ceremony:
Everyone gathered in the small hall to witness the ceremony. Tracy and Tim had written the script themselves using a medieval version of the language. Tracy's sister who acted as celebrant for the day, officiated as the couple made their vows to one another and exchanged rings. The homage ceremony steeped in history followed, in which the bride and groom in turn collected a small amount of honey from a bowl and using a silver spoon fed one another. They drank mead from a goblet that afterwards was passed among the guests with the invitation to do likewise.

Using a quill Tim and Tracy signed the special book in which the words of the ceremony had been written, the guests were also invited to add their names and a message.

Refreshments:
A gong sounded, announcing that the banquet was about to begin. The bridal pair with their guests moved into the Great Hall. Here the building had been transformed with tapestries, flags, hangings and a pair of stocks that were used later in the evening and provided some amusing photographs. The flickering candlelight added a sense of mystery to the setting. It was like stepping back into a bygone age. Arrangements of fragrant lilies, lilac and tulips filled every ancient stone ledge.

Long wooden tables were laid traditionally with goblets, wooden platters and daggers. Bowls of pomegranates, dates and nuts doubled as table decorations, to be eaten with the selection of cheeses that followed the meal.

Minstrels sang Grace and continued to entertain throughout the evening.

The Menu was as follows:

- Thick vegetable soup with chunks of crusty bread.
- Roast haunch of venison.
- Herbed jacket potatoes.
- A rustic vegetable selection.
- Apple and quince pie or peach flummery.
- English cheeses.

Wenches circulated with jugs of ale while a jester and tumbler provided additional entertainment.

Cake and Speeches:
Goblets were refilled in readiness for the speeches. The best man recited some rather unrefined poetry that encouraged Tim in his speech to offer

a toast to lost friendship.

Tracy said a few words in which she thanked her sister who had been at her side all day.

Tracy and Tim cut the two-tier wedding cake with a dagger. Covered with marzipan the cakes were decorated with gilded fruits, flowers and leaves, and supported by a thick central stone pillar,

Entertainment:
The minstrels continued to play until late but with modern instruments and music for dancing.

Departure:
Having bid their guests good night, Tracy and Tim were driven home by friends.

Notes:
The invitations were designed and supplied by The Medieval Scribe.
Tel: 01580 211383
E-mail: websales@medievalscribe.com

Authentic props and table wear were hired from Belltower Enterprises.
Tel: 01372 277703

FAMILY AFFAIR

A Unitarian Church wedding followed by a picnic for forty adults, thirty children and three dogs.

Combining two families of four into one extended unit success-fully was challenging and suggested that the aim for the day should be to include each family member in as many ways as they wished. The day was organised their way, according to their budget and needs.

Action Plan:
The children were first to know of Zac and Sara's intention to marry, which would unite their lives and families and the reasons for their decision were explained. The couple obtained legal ad-vice concerning aspects that might affect their offspring.

Sara particularly wanted a church wedding and was aware that her divorced status would not present a problem to a Minister of the Unitarian Church. Zac, a widower, did not believe in God but preferred to embrace the Spirit of Life, which a free church acknowledges.

The Unitarian Minister met the family several times and between them they created a personal and meaningful ceremony, which in-cluded the children. By special request it was agreed that the wedding would take place on a Sunday after the morning service. The Minister advised them to follow the legal formalities and obtain the necessary certificate that she would require before the ceremony could take place.

As the couple had only a modest budget many friends offered to take responsibility for various aspects of the day. This emphasised the necessity to clarify everyone's role, which was as follows:

- Joe ordered the drinks and disposable glasses.
- Fay and Alun organised a games programme and the equipment required.
- Sue and Dave brought coals and master-minded the barbecue.

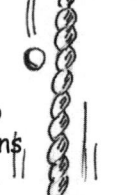

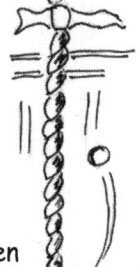

- Den took responsibility for providing sacks for rubbish and leaving the site clean and tidy.
- Sally took care of the bits and pieces; first aid kit, spare loo rolls, a bowl for hand washing with soap and towels, kitchen roll and cling film, wet wipes, scissors, string and sellotape.

Invitations:
With shared participation in mind the youngest family member drew a picture that was used for the wedding invitations. Guests were asked to wear suitable clothes for a picnic, and to bring rug or garden chairs, plate and knife and fork. Well-behaved dogs on leads were also welcomed.

Hen and Stag parties:
Zac offered to look after the children while Sara met with friends at one of their homes where they enjoyed a cosy evening with a lap supper, plenty of wine and a video of 'The Full Monty'.

Another evening Sara looked after the brood giving Zac the opportunity to spend an evening at the pub with his friends and the dartboard.

Bridal Wear:
Sara chose a two-piece outfit in beige linen; the slim fitting dress with a square neckline complemented the beautiful locket that was her wedding gift from Zac. Both dress and jacket were trimmed with simple embroidered motifs. She wore a hat that toned perfectly. The entire outfit had been purchased through the internet. Sara carried a posy of multi-coloured garden flowers tied with ribbons.

Groom's Wear:
For the wedding Zac wore a lounge suit with a carefully chosen tie that toned with Sara's posy.

Attendants:
Dressed in their favourite clothes, the children felt relaxed and happy.

Marriage Ceremony:
Having rehearsed previously, everyone knew exactly what to do. On the great day both families walked to church together to attend the morning service. Following this, the children processed to the front and turned to face the congregation. Sara and Zac followed them as 'Greensleeves' was played on the organ.

The service took place as follows:

- Welcome and introduction.
- Hymn, 'Morning has Broken'.
- A reading by friend Joy.
- Wedding address.
- The congregation were invited to join hands as the Minister said the following words. "We join hands to celebrate our humanness and the fact that we are connected to one another. A marriage always signifies the creation of a family. In the spirit of coming together as one family, we join hands to affirm the marriage of Sara and Zac".
- The couple wrote their own vows, which included the formal sentences required by law. Each child was mentioned by name and promised care by Zac and Sara.
- Blessing and exchange of rings.
- The Minister invited each child to light a candle that had been placed within easy reach on a low table, as a part of the symbolic ceremony.
- Sara and Zac then lit their candles joining flames with the children before lighting the candle of unity, uniting it in love.
- The signing of the marriage register was witnessed by the congregation.
- The Minister had previously encouraged each child to make a promise; these were recorded in a special book to symbolise their ongoing contribution to family life.
- Blessing the couple was followed by an invitation to kiss at which everyone spontaneously stood and applauded.
- Sara and Zac led the way down the aisle as the united family and guests followed. A selection of music was played which included 'The Teddy Bears' Picnic'.

The children's friends waited eagerly with bubble-making machines to bombard the newly bonded family as they stepped outside the church.

Photography:
Photographs were the responsibility of Zac's eldest son who had recently attended a photographic course and for the occasion he used his father's camera. After a few formal photographs had been taken many guests returned home to change before the picnic, but the camera would be in action again later.

The Setting:
Zac hired a public area in a beautiful woodland setting from the local council. This offered barbecue facilities, trees for hide-and-seek and a flat grassy area that was ideal for playing rounders. Some shelter was available as well as a standpipe, toilets and car parking facilities.

Drinks:
Some of the men took responsibility for pouring the drinks, which were served in disposable cups for reasons of safety. Scrumpy, wine and beer were available for the adults with a choice of soft and fizzy drinks served with long straws for the children.

The country and western band had been busking in the street when Zac first heard them play. Today they were looking as though they had just stepped out of a wild west movie playing tirelessly throughout the afternoon.

Refreshments:
To cut costs I agreed just to deliver the food. When the van pulled to a halt the barbecue was already glowing. Many hands unloaded marinated chicken drumsticks, bangers, home made kebabs and burgers, all of which were to be cooked by the guests. Bowls of salad and hedgehog rolls with butter completed the spread as everyone rallied to help lay out the picnic.

An ice-cream van had been pre-booked and called at an agreed time with pudding. The extensive selection of ice creams caused quite a dilemma.

Cake and Speeches:
Sara's eldest daughter had made dozens of cup cakes iced in different colours, decorated with love hearts and piled high on trays, which she and her friends handed round.

Zac's brother made a speech, based on Aesop's Fables. His observation of character was outstanding and provided much laughter. Finally he asked everyone to raise their glasses regardless of the contents and join with him in a toast to the newly formed family, mentioning each member by name.

Entertainment:
A box of simple outdoor toys and games was produced for those who wanted to play and teams were swiftly organised. Others went into the woodland on a prepared treasure hunt. The highlight of the afternoon was a dads' tug of war followed by a rather less strenuous one by the mums. The fun and games went on well into the evening but before nightfall the site was left clean and tidy.

Departure:
The newlyweds hardly had a romantic departure in cars loaded with picnic debris and tired children. Predictably the vehicle was covered in shaving foam and toilet paper with a miscellaneous assortment of items attached to the rear bumper that clattered behind them down the road.

Gifts:
The last thing on Zac and Sara's minds had been wedding presents but wonderful surprises kept arriving.

A group of friends clubbed together and gave the family a fully equipped wicker picnic basket that included a bottle of champagne.

A voucher for supper for two at a popular local restaurant was received with the additional offer of child sitting.

A day out for the whole family at a local farm centre, featuring tractor rides, pig racing, close contact with animals, opportunities to climb on stacked hay bales and rides of all descriptions.

Notes:
Revd. Johanne Boeke, Unitarian Minister, gave guidance with planning the ceremony.

THE SKY'S THE LIMIT

A cathedral wedding, that was followed by a formal marquee reception for two hundred and fifty guests.

To cater for a society wedding where clients were not working to a tight budget was a delightful experience for me. On this occasion mobile kitchen units, luxurious toilet facilities and an effective public address system were hired, together with quality china, silver and glassware. The addition of a toastmaster who would co-ordinate the proceedings ensured that every aspect of the day was managed with dignity, experience and good humour.

Proposal:
Jonathan organised a sky sign writer to fly over the remote holiday resort where he and Suzanne were staying. One morning the small aircraft appeared trailing a banner with the message 'MARRY ME SU'. Later that evening he slipped an ice cube containing a diamond ring into her drink.

Action Plan:
The official announcement of their engagement appeared in a national newspaper. Both having been brought up with traditional family values these were reflected in the wedding arrangements.

Jonathan and Suzanne made an appointment at the cathedral with the Dean to discuss the service and arrangements for their wedding.

Jonathan checked that I held public liability insurance. He also decided to take out an insurance policy to cover the wedding, should the unexpected happen.

Invitations:
Formal wedding invitations bearing the family crest were sent out well in advance by Suzanne's parents, giving guests a chance to put the date into their dairies, requesting that they respond by a

given date. The cream and silver theme introduced by the invitations was reflected throughout the wedding.

After a great deal of contemplation Suzanne and Jonathan decided to include children in the arrangements. An additional slip was added to the appropriate invitations informing guests with children that crèche facilities would be available.

For wedding presents the couple used the services of a large department store. This arrangement was convenient for guests to order gifts by telephone, fax or e-mail and have them gift wrapped and delivered at an agreed time, place and date.

Hen and Stag Parties:
Two of Suzanne's friends knew how anxious she was to look her best for the wedding. They arranged a special pre-nuptial work out for all three of them. They also hired the services of a personal trainer to keep her motivated and striving towards realistic goals.

Jonathan and his friends, who were pilots in the same squadron, met in the officers' mess for drinks before a hired minibus took them to a restaurant for dinner where a surprise was awaiting him in the shape of a female strip-o-gram.

Bridal Wear:
Suzanne wore a cream gown with a long train decorated with silver embroidery and pearls. Her 'something old' was the veil and headdress that her mother had worn at her own wedding which had been stored carefully in acid free tissue. To complement her height she carried a cascading bouquet of cream and white roses, orchids, freesia, lilies, green hydrangea and trails of fern.

Groom's Wear:
Jonathan and his best man wore their number one uniforms with dress swords. Other members of the wedding party wore dark morning suits with silver waistcoats and cream ties, completed by a single orchid in their buttonholes.

Attendants:
Jonathan's sister, who was maid of honour, dressed in a full-length silver satin dress with matching shoes. She carried a hand-tied bouquet of cream roses, freesia and green hydrangea.

The six small bridesmaids wore ankle-length dresses of cream silk chiffon with silver sashes and delicate silver necklaces with heart shaped pendants that were gifts from the bride and groom. Their flowers echoed the cream and silver theme and included dainty sprigs of gypsophila, which had been silvered, adding a twinkle when catching the light. This touch made Suzanne's day reflecting her secret love of the glitz.

Transport:
Prepared for rain or shine, the Victorian carriage, drawn by a pair of greys arrived in good time to first transport the bridesmaids to the cathedral, returning the short distance for the bride and her father. The driver and groom wearing black livery drew the stately pair to a halt at the Cathedral entrance, getting the bride there traditionally late but by only half a minute.

Marriage Ceremony:
Many of Suzanne's ancestors had married in the Cathedral and she wished to continue this family tradition. Banks of cream flowers with touches of green and silver flanked the aisle while similar posies adorned the pew ends.

Two trumpeters heralded the arrival of the bride who walked up the long nave on her father's arm to the magnificent march from Verdi's 'Aida' followed by her six small bridesmaids who carried her train. Finally her maid of honour completed the procession.

A traditional marriage ceremony was performed by the Dean:
- Welcome and introduction.
- Hymn: 'Love Divine, all Loves Excelling'.
- Reading.
- Wedding Address.
- Vows.
- Blessing and exchange of rings.
- During the registration of marriage a friend sang: 'Oh Perfect Love', with choral and organ accompaniment.
- The composer played a piece on the organ that he had written especially for the occasion.
- The pronouncement of marriage.
- Blessing.

The recessional procession moved slowly down the aisle as the organ and trumpets played Jeremiah Clarke's 'Trumpet Voluntary'. At the great west door a guard of honour awaited them, twelve members of the groom's squadron, their swords held high formed an archway under which the couple passed.

The coach and pair were waiting to transport the newlyweds the short distance to the reception that was to be held in a marquee erected in the grounds of the famous public school that Jonathan had attended. On the way they enjoyed a bottle of complimentary champagne provided by the carriage company.

Photography:
A well-known photographer had shown them portfolios of previous weddings that he had photographed, as did the video maker who had won several prestigious awards.

Having passed beneath the old flint archway into the cobbled yard the newlyweds were driven past the many ancient buildings to a large marquee that was erected on the lawns. Much of the formal photography took place using the graceful and historic, cloistered buildings as a backdrop, stirring feelings of nostalgia within Jonathan and his old school friends.

Drinks:
A repertoire of classical music was played on a harp, the silvery notes carried, without drowning conversation. The toastmaster wearing his traditional red tailcoat announced the arrival of each guest by name to be received by the bride, groom and their respective parents. Champagne cocktails and canapés were served and guests waiting in the long receiving line were not forgotten.

The Setting:
Large stone urns overflowing with white blooms decorated the marquee; roses, phlox, delphinium, gladioli, stocks and lilies. Poles wrapped in yards of shimmering silver fabric were garlanded and festooned with flowers and foliage. A collaboration of flowers formed a backdrop to a raised dais where the wedding cake was displayed. Two human statues, painted from head to toe in silver body paint stood either side and occasionally jerked into life.

Refreshments:
Wines for this special occasion bore individually designed labels that were printed with a small photograph of Suzanne and Jonathan with the wedding date and location on the front label. The wording on the back was as follows: 'Suzanne and Jonathan's Wedding Wine is a blend of two superb grapes. It combines the finest produce from the Sussex and Hampshire regions and will mature delightfully with time. This excellent vintage will always ensure a great reception'.

The Toastmaster drew attention to the well-displayed table plans as the ushers assisted guests in finding their seats. A silver luggage label tied with ribbon to each chair back identified the place setting.

The Dean said Grace before the meal.

"For what we are about to receive, may the Lord make us truly thankful."

The menu featured mainly local produce and was as follows:

- Trout and watercress mousse wrapped in filo pastry served with hollandaise sauce.
- Roast haunch of venison, port wine jus and heart shaped croutons.
- Medley of fresh vegetables.
- A trio of tiny puddings.
- Coffee and silver wrapped heart shaped mints.

Cake and Speeches:
When glasses of champagne had been distributed, the toastmaster announced and co-ordinated the cake cutting and speeches.

The intricate five-tier cake bore the crests of both families and the interwoven initials of the couple. Jonathan drew his ceremonial sword and posed with his wife for photographs of the cake cutting ceremony. The first slice of cake was easily removed by means of a ribbon. Within the cavity the couple discovered a tiny box containing two keys marked with their initials.

The father of the bride began his speech by welcoming the bride and groom, family and friends, ladies and gentlemen. He continued by telling a few amusing anecdotes about his daughter, complimenting her on her appearance and mentioned his pleasure at escorting her up the aisle. Finally he asked that glasses be raised "To the happy couple, Suzanne and Jonathan."

The groom thanked his in-laws and his own parents for all they had done to make the day such a success. He also thanked the bridesmaids, his best man and the ushers. A few carefully chosen one-liners followed.

The best man thanked the groom on behalf of the bridesmaids for his kind words. In his speech he referred to several stories and world events that occurred on the day of Jonathan and Suzanne's births. Having taken the appropriate information from the pages, he gave them the newspapers as a souvenir.

Entertainment:
To capture the day everyone was invited to sign a large parchment on which the couple's names, the date and venue was written in traditional calligraphy. Guests were asked to sign with a personal message for the couple, when completed, the artwork was replaced into its handmade frame.

Departure:
Suzanne and Jonathan left by helicopter later in the evening for a secret honeymoon destination.

Gifts:
The keys found in the wedding cake fitted a Porsche for Jonathan and BMW sports car for Suzanne, both with personalised number plates. They were gifts from Jonathan's parents.

Notes:
Careful planning ensured that the couple and their future family were as well protected as possible from the problems that life can throw. Allied Professional Will Writers Limited maintain a register of local financial advisers and will writers.
Tel: 0845 166 8873

The tiny white gypsophila flowers had been dipped into glue and then into silver glitter to achieve the sparkly effect.

Wedding insurance.
Website: www.insurancewide.co

Celebration Wines with personalised labels.
Tel: 028 90 20 70 50
Website: www.celebrationwines.co.uk

Crèche facilities and party tables for the children with plenty of care, fun and games were provided by:
Daisy Daisy.
Tel: 01279 410 908
Website: www.daisyweddingcreches.co.uk

Remember When Newspapers.
Tel: 020 8763 6363
Website: www.remember-when.co.uk

Jonathan booked a one-to-one session with a professional scriptwriter to ensure that the appropriate etiquette was followed in his speech and that his one-liners were funny.
E-mail: robertalanhaven@onetel.com

Framed Parchments.
Website: www.carpediem.co.uk

ROSE GARDEN

A ceremony of commitment followed by tea for forty guests in a beautiful rose garden.

When a friend's daughter asked me for ideas for her special day, it was with great pleasure that I put on my 'thinking cap'. In her late teens Sally found her spiritual path that now formed a vital part of her personality. A conventional wedding seemed inappropriate as neither Sally nor Roy had been influenced by religion and they were fearful of making a legal commitment as both had divorced parents. A simple ceremony of commitment felt comfortable for them at this time. One day it might lead to a legal marriage. They were delighted as we began to plan their day their way and the 'Rose Garden' celebration eventually emerged.

Action Plan:
Roy and Sally wanted their ceremony of commitment to be unique to them without competition or commercialism. Together they drew up a pre-nuptial agreement that helped them to clarify their expectations within the relationship. They were also both aware that their commitment was not binding by law.

A date was booked with the celebrant to discuss the ceremony in detail.

Invitations:
A photograph of Roy and Sally decorated the front of the invitation in which an explanation of the occasion was given and a request made that guests respond by a given date.

Sally's Dress:
Sally's choice of dress was a long flowing kaftan in pale mauve and white patterned voile. She wore glass beads around her neck and flip-flops decorated with matching beads.

Roy's Dress:
Roy wore a light coloured cotton top and trousers, with a wooden medallion on a leather thong around his neck. He too wore flip-flops.

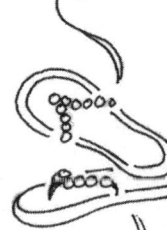

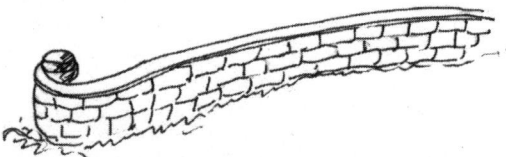

The Setting:
Sally and Roy were delighted when they found the beautiful walled rose garden and arbour that was full of colour and fragrance with well-tended lawns. A weatherworn pavilion with a covered terrace was also available for shelter should it be required.

Photography:
One after another candid camera shots were taken including many close-ups. The day was captured as it happened. Photographs taken both in black and white and colour were later displayed in an album and given as a practical gift to the couple by a relation.

The Ceremony:
The celebrant welcomed everybody into the garden and to the commitment ceremony of Sally and Roy. The assembled party formed a circle around the prettily clothed table on which was placed:

- A bowl of rose water and a towel.
- A crystal vase containing two long-stemmed white roses.
- Two white candles.
- A large piece of amethyst on which two silver bracelets lay.
- A handcrafted book from which the celebrant read.

The couple's hands were ceremoniously washed in rose water, having been cleansed of their past lives both were now symbolically free. As they had learned the words by heart Sally and Roy were able to look into each other's eyes as they made promises to one another. The exchange of bracelets followed, each engraved with a personal message. After the prayer that called on the natural world to bless their union, Roy, Sally and two friends who acted as witnesses signed the certificate in the book. Following the pronouncement of their union, the couple embraced and the celebrant presented them each with a single white rose. They then exchanged blooms as their symbol of love for one another. The celebrant asked that on this day every year they exchange a similar bloom, also whenever they have difficulty in finding words to resolve certain issues. The rose being a statement and a request for a little extra loving care. Finally everyone joined hands for a blessing. The celebrant congratulated Sally and Roy and asked guests to sign the book and write a personal message to the couple.

Drinks:
The children blew bubbles as the string quartet played with gusto 'Zing Went the Strings of My Heart' and continued with music from the shows. Tall glasses of Pimm's were served, full of fruit, ice, mint and sprigs of borage with its bright blue star-shaped flowers.

Refreshments:
Trays of appetising delicacies were handed around as guests strolled in the scented garden. The selection included tiny cucumber and smoked salmon sandwiches, asparagus rolls, cheese and sesame straws and a hollowed pineapple filled with cream cheese and surrounded with strawberries for dunking. Baskets of small cakes, meringues, macaroons, chocolate éclairs, shortbread and fresh fruit threaded onto glitter sticks were circulated. When the chunks of fruit had been eaten the glitter sticks were stuck into the lawn, twinkling in the sunlight like multi-coloured daisies. Welcome cups of tea were served from the pavilion including a selection of fruit and flower teas.

Sally, her mother and aunt had prepared the food, hiring students from the local college to undertake the service.

Cake and Speeches:
Glasses of well-chilled sparkling wine were handed out. Guests gathered around the passion cake made by Sally's mother that was decorated with white frosting and crystallised rose petals. Together the couple cut the first slice as guests raised their glasses.

Sally's stepfather, in his brief speech, congratulated the pair, affirming his pleasure at Sally's choice of a partner. He continued by saying some loving words and telling a few amusing stories about her.

In return Roy thanked Sally's parents for making him so welcome and referred to his and Sally's horoscope readings and their compatibility.

Departure:
Having spent a wonderful afternoon with their family and friends the couple left briefly to change in readiness for going away. They returned on a tandem wearing shorts and T-shirts with backpacks in preparation for their touring holiday.

Gifts:
Sally's mother compiled a collection of recipes for her daughter that included the passion cake which had always been a family favourite.

Three exquisitely hand-worked tapestry cushions with a different rose design on each was a gift from Sally's aunt.

Notes:
The ceremony was written and conducted by a celebrant trained by Choice Ceremonies.
Tel: 023 8086 1256
Website: www.choiceceremonies.co.uk

Glitter sticks for the fruit kebabs are obtainable by telephoning Bill and Car.
Tel: 01322 273330

To order the handcrafted book contact Taryn.
Tel: 023 8086 1256.

SWAN LAKE

A traditional service of marriage in an historic chapel that was followed by a reception for fifty guests.

Helping to arrange and cater for this wedding reminded me of my early years working at the Royal Opera House, Covent Garden. Swan Lake was the first production in which I was involved in making the costumes. It was exciting to see my own work on stage for the first time.

Action Plan:
Lee eventually plucked up enough courage to invite Amanda to a performance of Swan Lake. Later when planning their wedding they decided to use the memory of this first date as the theme.

The church and reception facilities were booked at a stately home that was set in forty acres of beautiful countryside including a lake with swans. The reception rooms were available for hire with the option of choosing their own caterers. This offered a perfect setting for the wedding with a unique chapel that was registered for marriages.

Amanda and Lee visited the local Rector who explained the legalities surrounding marriage, including the need to publish their banns for three Sundays in the parish in which each party lived.

Invitations:
Amanda personalised standard wedding invitations with a white feather inserted between two diagonal slots that emphasised the theme for the wedding. She also enclosed a list of local hotels and bed and breakfast accommodation.

Rather than risk receiving six toasters: 'The Wedding List Poem' was enclosed with the invitation, which in a tactful way conveyed the message that cheques would be preferable to presents.

There is nothing wrong with toasters
Though it should be said
A dozen in the kitchen
Takes an awful lot of bread.

So please don't think us cheeky

If gifts we'd rather choose
Not put away in drawers
But actually want to use.

So leave behind the presents
At this our wedding bash
We'd love to have your company
But wouldn't mind the cash!

By Sharon Miller

Hen and Stag Parties:
For her hen night Amanda was wined and dined in style at a top London restaurant by three close friends.

Lee spent the weekend fly-fishing and was given a pair of waders and a landing net as a gift to encourage him to continue the sport. The catch of the day was later cooked during a boozy supper at a friend's flat.

Bridal Wear:
Amanda's engagement ring was set with her birthstone, a pale blue aquamarine that influenced the colour she chose to wear for her wedding. The crepe backed satin two-piece with beaded detail on the jacket was worn over a slim fitting floor-length dress. She added a white feather boa and on her head a diamond tiara.

Groom's Wear:
Lee and his best man, Tom, chose grey morning suits with top hats. Their waistcoats reflected the colour of Amanda's dress, as did their matching cravats. White camellias in their buttonholes completed their ensembles.

Attendants:
Lee's three-year-old nephew acted as pageboy wearing grey trousers and waistcoat with an aquamarine silk shirt.

Transport:
A beribboned white vintage Rolls Royce transported Amanda and her brother in style to the wedding.

The Setting:
The undulating countryside surrounding the stately home provided wonderful views as the car drove through the deer park and past the lake.

Marriage Ceremony:
At the entrance to the chapel stood a pedestal of all white flowers containing lilac blossoms, tulips, iris and boughs from the snowball tree. Two smaller versions of the same arrangement were placed on the altar.

Lee arrived with his best man and several friends half an hour before the service began. Order of service sheets were handed out by the pageboy as guests arrived and were directed to their pews. While awaiting the arrival of the bride, they admired the many unique and fascinating features of the chapel.

The harpist played and Lee turned to greet his beautiful bride as she made her way up the aisle escorted by her brother. A traditional ceremony of marriage took place in which Amanda promised to love and honour Lee. In turn Lee made the same promises to Amanda. Both rings tied with ribbon to a small and decorative cushion were handed to the vicar by the pageboy to be blessed. Prayers and readings followed. The service ended with the newlyweds pledging to renew their vows annually before signing the marriage register. Amanda and Lee followed by their families and friends made their way down the short aisle to music from Swan Lake.

After the service, in spite of the chill air, the wedding party walked through the ancient walled garden pausing for photographs on their way towards the warmth of the reception rooms.

Photographs:
Lee booked the photographer whose work he and Amanda had often admired. The best man organised guests into groups in a systematic way using a list of required shots to be taken. Not surprisingly, a Saturday in March was chilly and everyone appreciated the speed and skill with which the formal photographs were completed.

Drinks:
The harpist, now relocated, continued to play in the reception hall as guests were served glasses of hot mulled white wine; heated white wine to which a dash of brandy, orange and lemon zest, sugar and spices had been added.

Refreshments:
The dining room was decorated with all white flower arrangements in which swathes of aquamarine voile and a few large white feathers had been incorporated.

Everyone relaxed at prettily laid circular tables clothed in white, the matching napkins were folded into the shape of water lilies, each one holding a bread roll. The tables were decorated with simple but effective centrepieces. Thick white candles that burned within blocks of ice had been placed in shallow glass dishes on mirror tiles that doubled the impact, this surprising combination of ice and fire burned for many hours.

At Christmas while shopping in a garden centre, a tiny glass church with a sparkly snow-covered roof caught Amanda's eye. She purchased one for each place setting attaching the names of guests. The idea delighted her knowing that the mementoes would decorate the trees of her friends at Christmas for many years to come.

The printed menus offered the following:

- Mushroom and herb tarts.
- Fillets of salmon with a tarragon sauce garnished with baby vegetables.
- Minted new potatoes.
- Side salad.

A buffet garlanded with delicate smilax fern and swathes of tulle bore a generous selection of desserts. Every shape, colour, texture and flavour imaginable was available for guests to choose whatever they fancied. A spectacular centrepiece was a pair of ice swans displayed on a decorated mirror. Their beaks touched forming a heart shape and their hollowed backs contained an exotic fruit salad. The meal ended with handmade chocolates served with coffee.

Cake and Speeches:
In his speech Amanda's brother welcomed guests from near and far and told a few amusing stories about his 'baby sister'. Wishing the newlyweds much happiness, he proposed a toast to the bride and groom.

Lee began his speech by mentioning that it happened to be his wife's birthday. Everyone joined him in singing 'happy birthday' followed by three cheers for the bride. He gave a short history of their relationship, how they met and their reasons for choosing the romantic Swan Lake theme for their wedding. The idea being based on the fact that swans mate for life.

Looking almost too beautiful to eat, the three-tier cake iced in the palest shade of aquamarine was decorated with delicate sugar flowers and lacework. The top tier, which displayed a pair of swans, was not cut but kept intact, hopefully for a christening.

Entertainment:
On each table was a small box of Table Trivia containing question and answer cards for guests to use in a light-hearted way.

Departure:
As dusk was falling the newly married couple took their leave. The Rolls drove down the winding driveway, past the lake and out of sight with an old boot bumping along behind them, for luck.

Gifts:
A friend ordered a bottle of champagne, through the airline, that was served to Lee and Amanda on their honeymoon flight.

A swan was adopted for the couple through Abotsbury Swanlink in Weymouth.
Tel: 01305 871684

Notes:
'The Wedding List Poem' was written especially for the occasion by Sharon Miller 'The Verse Nurse'.
Tel: 01903 693100
E-mail: R.S.Miller@btinternet.com

Wedding Trivia cards and ideas for Hen and Stag nights were gleaned from:
Website: www.confetti.co.uk

For information on Iceometric ice carvings.
Tel: 07970 700070
Website: www.iceometric.co.uk
E-mail: info@iceometric.co.uk

Amanda later acknowledged gift cheques on paper decorated with digital images of their wedding day.

CHARITY FAYRE

*A traditional wedding followed by a tea dance reception
with a jazz band for one hundred guests.
The evening continued with a disco and African-style
finger buffet supper for one hundred and fifty.*

I can take little credit for the originality of this wedding. By
the time Mandy and Paul came to see me most of the arrangements had been made. As a family they had planned to do their
own catering but when the time drew near they were daunted
by the enormity of the task. Happily I was free to co-ordinate
the tea and to provide the evening buffet. I was also able to
admire and enjoy the uniqueness of the occasion.

Proposal:
It was Easter Saturday as Mandy awaited Paul's arrival for
afternoon tea on the terrace of a country house hotel. For
her recent birthday he had given her a dishwasher, which
she wished had been a ring and to her irritation today he
was late, which didn't help matters. Her thoughts were
distracted when she noticed someone on horseback galloping
towards her along a tree-lined avenue. Paul's dramatic arrival
bearing an engagement ring changed everything.

Action Plan:
Paul and Mandy met while taking part in a fashion show in aid of
Oxfam, a charity that they both supported. Wishing to share
the happiness of their big day with those less fortunate, the
couple asked family and friends to help raise funds for Oxfam
while celebrating their wedding.

The wedding was to take place in Mandy's parish church. The
couple made an appointment with the minister to check the
availability of their chosen date, and make the necessary
arrangements to book the organist and choir and for the
banns to be called.

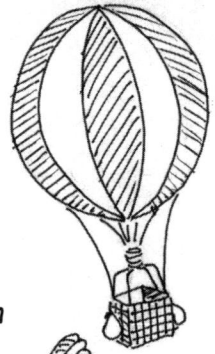

Invitations:
The invitations contained an information sheet giving a timed programme of events. A brief summary followed telling how Paul and Mandy met and included the following request:

'We hope that you can find time to participate in our unusual idea. We believe that as well as doing some small amount of good, it will also add to the enjoyment of the day.'

The fundraising plan was as follows:

- The groom and guests (the bride and bridesmaid excluded) were asked to buy all or part of their outfits from any Oxfam shop with the emphasis on being glamorous or fun. Guests were requested to bring their receipts of purchase and the total amount of money spent would be added up and announced during the reception.
- Drinks would be plentiful but guests were asked to bring a supply of fifty pence pieces as donations, providing another opportunity to raise funds.
- The host and hostess were available for hire (dances only or subject to negotiation) throughout the evening. Guests were advised to book early to avoid disappointment.

Bridal Wear:
Mandy wore a sleek gown of white slipper satin with a large fabric bow attached to the removable train and a short purple velvet jacket. Her shoulder-length veil was held in place with a delicate gold filigree and diamond tiara. Within her armful of beautiful regale lilies a few stems of purple statice reflected the colour of her jacket.

Groom's Wear:
Paul continued his equestrian theme by wearing black riding breeches and jacket with a gold waistcoat. His riding boots were brown, which was easily explained by his shopping limitations!

Attendant:
The little bridesmaid wore a white three-quarter-length dress with puffed sleeves and carried a posy of purple anemones.

Transport:
Mandy travelled to church with her father in a white taxi decorated with ribbons.

Photography:
Paul and Mandy decided to have formal photographs taken at the church that included some classic poses and portraits. Photographs of guests as they arrived for the service were taken, while others throughout the day

were as spontaneous as the photographer chose to make them, which included Mandy's earlier preparations.

Marriage Ceremony:
Spring was in the air. Arrangements of purple tulips, lilac, iris, white narcissus and gold and white lilies decorated the church.

Mandy and her father walked up the aisle as the organist played 'The Bridal March' by Wagner.

The service began with the hymn 'Love Divine' and was followed by a traditional marriage ceremony interwoven with prayers and readings:

- During the signing of the register a solo was sung by a member of the choir, Psalm 23 'The Lord is my Shepherd'.
- The recessional procession formed behind the newly married couple as 'The Wedding March' by Mendelssohn was played and the church bells pealed joyfully.

When the photographs had been taken, Mandy, Paul and their guests strolled the short distance across the crocus studded green to where the reception was taking place.

The Setting:
The heady perfume of lilies filled the hall; dramatic floral displays were enhanced with golden cherubs that were the remains of a shop window display retrieved from a skip by Mandy. This splendid find confirmed the regal purple, gold and white theme for the wedding.

Full of character, the old hall reflected hints of faded glory but had a perfect floor for dancing and a well equipped, modernised kitchen. When using the cloakrooms, guests appreciated Mandy's thoughtful touches in providing vases of flowers, soft towels and baskets of toiletries.

Guests' Dress:
Guests had chosen an intriguing collection of outfits that had been purchased from Oxfam shops. Some aimed for elegant sophistication while others had clearly enjoyed every moment of their shopping experience, dressing with taste and imagination. On arrival, receipts of purchase were placed as requested into a box.

Drinks:
Corks popped and champagne flowed as Mandy and Paul welcomed their guests while the jazz band played in the background.

Paul swept Mandy across the floor for the first dance to the tune of 'It Had To Be You'. With her train removed the dramatic knee high slit in the back of her dress was revealed.

Refreshments:
The seating arrangements for tea were casual. Food was displayed on three adjoining circular tables that were clothed to the floor and garlanded with trails of ivy with the wedding cake forming a centrepiece. A friend of Mandy's had made a vast array of beautifully decorated small cakes that were set on gold doilies with purple flower heads strewn among the display. A selection of teas was served.

Cake and Speeches:
Mandy's father congratulated the newlyweds and asked everyone to join him and his wife in a toast to "Mandy and Paul".

Paul complimented his beautiful bride and the bridesmaid on their appearance and continued by thanking the guests for the obvious trouble they had taken in purchasing their outfits. He mentioned that the grand total raised in support of Oxfam, as a direct result of their shopping sprees would be announced later in the evening.

Full of anecdotes, the best man's speech followed. The laughter became infectious when he began to talk about Paul's menagerie of unusual pets. The dogs, ferrets and many varieties of birds of prey gave him plenty of scope. When the laughter had subsided a little he asked "Will you please raise your glasses to Mandy and Paul?" Glasses of bubbly were raised yet again, followed by the bride and groom cutting the wedding cake.

The rich fruit cake iced in white was heavily decorated with swags and tails of purple and gold fondant icing with golden cherubs supporting each of the three tiers.

Evening Party:
Paul purchased the drinks on a sale or return basis from a supermarket, which included the hire of the necessary glasses. During the evening, wine, beer and soft drinks were available as additional guests arrived for the disco. Drinks were served and donations of fifty pence per glass were made, which boosted the fundraising campaign yet again.

Refreshments:
It was a joy to arrange the savoury finger buffet for the evening based on an African safari theme. The food was presented in leaf-lined baskets and incorporated my collection of carved wooden animals, treasures from my own recent visit to Kenya. The African theme linked with the couple's mutual love of wildlife and their forthcoming safari honeymoon.

At the end of the evening Mandy and Paul left the reception wearing safari outfits.

Gifts:
A group of Mandy and Paul's friends clubbed together to give them a once in a lifetime experience while on honeymoon: An early morning, hot air balloon flight, with the opportunity to view herds of wild animals while moving silently above. The flight concluded with a champagne breakfast in the middle of nowhere.

A copy of the Oxfam fashion show programme at which the couple met was mounted and framed, making it a nostalgic gift.

Notes:
Despite the florist's diligence when preparing the lilies, there is always a risk of the pollen staining, so reels of sticky tape were placed in the cloakrooms with a note attached explaining how to remove the bright yellow pollen from clothes should they become marked. Guests were advised not to dampen the fabric but simply lift the pollen away with the sticky tape.

OVER THE RAINBOW

A traditional church wedding and reception for seventy guests that included a few Canadian touches.

Wendy and her Canadian partner, Jim, arranged their wedding a year in advance but due to the tragic death of Wendy's grandparents they almost cancelled everything. Following our discussion the couple reconsidered and decided to continue with their plans adopting a theme that would pay tribute to their loved ones.

Action Plan:
Wendy and Jim's engagement had been interspersed with laughter and tears. This suggested a time of sunshine and showers that symbolised a rainbow, which became the theme for their multi-coloured wedding.

The couple made arrangements to visit the minister at Wendy's local church to confirm their chosen date and talk about the ceremony. As the day drew nearer they revisited to discuss the calling of the banns and make final decisions regarding the content of the service.

A rehearsal for the wedding party took place at the church, on the eve of the wedding.

Invitations:
The invitations incorporated a colourful three-dimensional pop-up rainbow and sparkling glitter was added to each envelope. It was clearly stated that children were welcome and that there would be a special buffet and entertainment provided for them. A stamped addressed envelope was enclosed for the reply, together with a map of the area and a list of local accommodation.

Stag and Hen Parties:
Rather than have separate parties Jim and Wendy arranged a dinner for both families. Jim's relations travelled from Canada for the wedding. It was the first time they had all met.

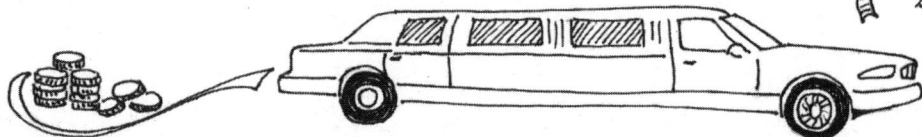

Bridal Wear:
Wendy's oyster satin wedding gown was designed and made by an aunt. The empire line dress was fastened at the back with forty-nine tiny fabric covered buttons, a number symbolising eternity. The skirt was decorated with teardrop crystals and matched those in her tiara that flashed and sparkled as they caught the sunlight. She wore a shoulder-length veil and carried a bouquet of flowers in a rainbow of colours. On this special day she wore her grandmother's engagement ring, together with her own on her right hand.

Groom's Wear:
The rainbow theme was carried through into the waistcoats worn by Jim, his best man and the ushers beneath their midnight blue frock coats. Jim wore the pocket watch that had belonged to Wendy's grandfather tucked into his waistcoat pocket.

Attendants:
The seven little bridesmaids were dressed in ankle-length dresses with puffed sleeves made from sky-blue dupion silk. Each sash took a different colour from the rainbow, red, orange, yellow, green, blue, indigo and violet. They carried baskets of mixed flowers that harmonised with their floral headdresses and the bride's bouquet.

Transport:
A white, stretched limousine decorated with brightly coloured ribbons transported the bridesmaids to church, returning for the bride and her father.

Photography:
A formal photo call was arranged but the couple were anxious to include a few candid camera shots to bring life into what could have been be a static album.

Marriage Ceremony:
The organ played as Wendy, escorted by her father and followed by the bridesmaids, walked up the aisle towards her husband-to-be. Jim moved to meet his bride, smiling with his arms outstretched.

As had been previously arranged the bridesmaids settled upon cushions that had been placed either side of the chancel steps, offering them a ringside view of the proceedings. They were given books to occupy them.

The Minister welcomed everybody. He started by explaining the concept of marriage in a simple way that the children could understand.

A traditional service of marriage was interspersed with personal contributions from family members which included:

- A flute solo.
- A Bible reading.
- A poem, which had been written especially for the occasion that helped to bridge the gap between sadness and joy:

'Sunshine and Showers'

Our hearts are tinged with sadness
For loved ones who have gone
But may it comfort you to know

Your grandparents look on.
So to family and to friends
Be sure, they are never far away,

And so with great affection
We remember them today.

It's been a time of mixed emotions
There've been smiles and there've been tears
And when the wedding seemed unlikely
You have pushed on through your fears.
If they were here in person
And could say a word or two
You know that they would want to send
Their joy and love to you.

At the end of every rainbow
Or so we have been told
Those who truly do believe
Will find a crock of gold.
Such treasure has been held today
By Wendy and by Jim
Now that he has found her
And now that she's found him.

By Sharon Miller.

During the signing of the marriage register the hymn 'Who Put the Colour in the Rainbow' was sung by all the children. The newlyweds walked down the aisle followed by their families and friends to 'Trumpet Time' by Henry Purcell. After the formal photographs had been taken and before leaving for the reception, Wendy placed her bouquet on her grandparents' grave.

The Setting:
The community centre was light and airy with modern conveniences. Tables were arranged in a horseshoe shape and clothed in pale blue damask with

deep blue serviettes. At intervals the bridesmaids' baskets were placed to anchor bunches of rainbow coloured helium filled balloons. Attached to ribbons of varying lengths they filled the high ceiling space transforming the sports hall. Each place setting was marked with a named cracker containing a golden hat, a riddle and party popper.

At the end of the rainbow we are led to believe, there is a crock of gold. This idea was interpreted by arranging a collection of golden blooms, gilded leaves and seed heads that cascaded from a large earthenware crock lying in the centre of the buffet. Gold wrapped chocolate coins tumbled onto the table, waiting to be eaten with coffee.

Drinks:
The bridal party formed a receiving line in the spacious hallway to greet the guests. Tall glasses of fruit punch were served, both alcoholic and non alcoholic, garnished with exotic fruits and plenty of crackling ice. A selection of light cocktail savouries was handed around as a pianist played a programme of music that continued throughout the reception.

Anxious that people might not mix, a clown was hired to break the ice should there be any and to entertain the children.

Refreshments:
Laminated lists displayed the seating plans. Assisted by the ushers, guests found their places in readiness for the meal. The best man asked that everyone be upstanding for the bride and groom as they entered the room hand in hand. The guests applauded spontaneously as the couple took their seats at the top table.

The best man said grace before the meal began.

When the starter had been cleared, Wendy and Jim with the rest of the bridal party were invited to the buffet to be served first, followed by guests in small groups thus avoiding queues.

The menu consisted of:
- Melon and raspberry cocktail.
- Poached Canadian salmon; its scales replicated with cucumber slices and glazed with aspic.
- A selection of cold meats.
- Quiche with various fillings.
- Herb bread, served hot.
- New potatoes in parsley butter.
- Arcs of rainbow salad arranged on oval trays followed the theme and were composed of; tomato slices, grated carrot, sweet corn, shredded lettuce. Red cabbage cooked without vinegar provided

the colour blue, some cooked with vinegar achieved the colour indigo and beetroot cubes mixed with mayonnaise completed the spectrum.
- Dessert was pecan and maple syrup tart made from a traditional Canadian recipe topped with whipped cream.

The children helped themselves from a low table containing all the food and drinks that children like best including a selection of ice creams. Plastic tableware was provided for safety.

When the meal was finished, the clown encouraged the youngsters into the small hall where they were entertained and shown how to model balloons into fascinating objects and shapes, returning when the formalities were complete.

Cake and Speeches:
Instead of a traditional wedding cake, a profusion of tiny cakes were distributed, each one a miniature work of art decorated with sugar flowers in rainbow colours.

Glasses of champagne were circulated in readiness for the toasts and speeches.

Wendy's father welcomed guests, especially those who had made long journeys from Vancouver, Toronto, and Calgary. He told a few gentle anecdotes about his daughter's cooking, wishing Jim the best of luck! He asked that everyone join him in a toast to the bride and groom, wishing them a long and happy marriage.

The bride's mother also said a few words of congratulation to her daughter and welcomed her new son-in-law into the family.

During his speech, Jim mentioned the family's sad loss but said how proud Wendy's grandparents would have been of their beautiful granddaughter today.

The best man, a longstanding friend of Jim's, asked guests to follow a Canadian tradition by clinking their glasses until the groom kissed the bride. Toast after toast followed, clinking glasses alternated with cheering as the newlyweds responded.

Entertainment:
As the speeches came to an end the pianist played 'Somewhere Over the Rainbow' and continued with a selection of sixties music. Coffee was served from the buffet and the chocolate money quickly consumed. This informal interlude also offered an opportunity for everyone to mix and mingle.

Departure:
Having changed into clothes for travelling, the newly married couple bid their guests farewell before leaving for their Canadian honeymoon. Their journey included a trip from Vancouver on the 'Rocky Mountaineer' ending with a visit to Niagara Falls where they witnessed the Falls bathed in beautiful rainbows!

Gifts:
A full set of crystal glassware was among the couple's treasured gifts.

Wendy and Jim gave each of the bridesmaids a book 'My Day as a Bridesmaid' by Caroline Plaistead, published by Bloomsbury.

Notes:
'Sunshine and Showers,' was written by Sharon Miller 'The Verse Nurse'.
Tel: 01903 693100
E-mail: R.S.Miller@btinternet.com

Hand painted silk waistcoats from The Silk Studio.
Tel/Fax: 01805 603010
E-mail: sue@silkstudio.co.uk
Website: www.silkstudio.co.uk

Wedding crackers from Forever Memories Ltd.
Tel: 01384 878111
Website: www.forevermemories.co.uk

Before booking their honeymoon the couple checked that their passports were up to date.

Wendy's practical Mum organized an emergency kit, which contained plasters, safety pins, needles and cotton; scissors, clear nail varnish and headache pills just in case there was a need.

GAY MAGIC

A midsummer celebration at dawn that included Druid rites followed by a champagne breakfast for twenty-four.

Carol and Pam contacted me regarding the catering for their celebration party. I was also able to introduce them to a celebrant who would help them co-ordinate a commitment ceremony together with some emotional support. Pam's parents were unaware of her relationship with Carol. The celebrant pointed out that having a ceremony behind their backs would in the long term cause much distress, indicating a lack of trust. She urged Pam to speak to her parents as soon as possible, which she did. They were surprised and shocked at the thought of a gay wedding but after a time realised that Pam was still the daughter they knew and loved. All that they had ever wanted was her happiness. They could not spoil this occasion for her.

Action Plan:
Having decided to commit themselves for life, Carol and Pam introduced one another to their respective families. The couple drew up a pre-nuptial agreement regarding property and finance, they also discussed their personal expectations within the relationship.

The Civil Partnership Bill became law on 5th December 2005 and from this date same sex couples have been able to legalise their partnership within a civil ceremony. Following legal requirements Pam and Carol gave notice to the authority in which they lived. The information given was posted in the public domain for the following fifteen days and then the Civil partnership could take place.

An earth-centred ceremony was arranged on the moors to celebrate both the Summer Solstice and the legalisation of their partnership.

A breakfast reception at home was to follow, which they hoped their parents would attend. Pam obtained a long-range weather forecast before finalising the outdoor arrangements.

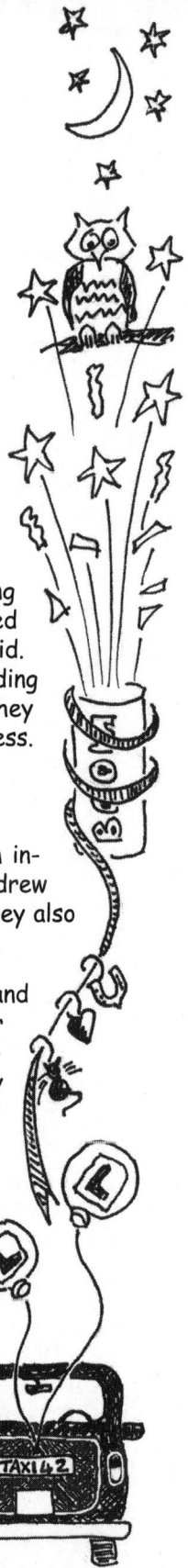

Invitations:
The purpose of the gathering was explained in the invitations that were hand-stencilled with a silhouette of an owl against a golden moon in a night sky. It was recommended that guests wear warm clothing and comfortable shoes as a night time walk was involved.

A note attached read, 'If you wish to give us a gift, we would appreciate DIY vouchers to buy materials for home refurbishment.' A scattering of gold star-shaped confetti accompanied each invitation.

Civil Ceremony:
The day before their celebration Pam and Carol went to the register office to sign a partnership schedule in front of the Superintendent Registrar, Registrar and two witnesses, which gave them the same legal rights as heterosexual couples.

Transport:
On the day of the party everyone travelled in a coach decorated with ribbons to a specified place on the moors, where permission had previously been granted by the landowner for the ceremony to take place.

Photography:
Pam and Carol's young neighbour who was studying videography and photography at college was delighted to experiment with a night-time shoot. He used a video camera and battery operated lamp with a defuser filter that created a soft, even light. During the ceremony he added a star burst filter to the lens that created a magical effect when focused on the lanterns and candles.

Bridal Wear:
Both brides wore oriental robes in rich shades of burgundy, orange and purple with co-ordinating cashmere wraps. They adopted an old custom from the Czech Republic by wearing a wreath of rosemary on their heads, a symbol of remembrance.

Commitment Ceremony:
Light from the lanterns glowed as the party walked to the appointed place where they sat and waited quietly for the rising sun whose eventual appearance created a breathtaking and sacred moment. In the glow of the breaking dawn the ceremony began as Carol and Pam cleansed their hands with water from the stream. The celebrant welcomed everyone into the presence, and continued by reading aloud the following words by Rumi:

Heart to Heart

'There is a way from your heart to mine
and my heart knows it,
because it is clean and pure like water.
When the water is still like a mirror
it can behold the moon.'

A circle was formed around a rock on which had been placed some candles and the rings. The celebrant called on the four elements symbolic to the Druid rite; fire, water, earth and air. Two candles were lit and passed around the circle, being placed finally on the central rock. From the flames the brides lit a third candle, symbolising their union. The group sat at peace as a beautiful spoken meditation took place until a small bell was tinkled. The ceremony continued with readings from 'The Prophet' by Kahlil Gibran before the celebrant called upon heaven and earth to witness the union. Pam and Carol found writing their own scripts to be a deeply moving experience in which they promised to commit themselves to each other's welfare and happiness in the years ahead. The exchange of rings followed and a loving cup containing mead was circulated among the friends, for each to take a sip.

The celebrant read the following:

A Benediction.

'Now, you will feel no rain,
for each of you will be shelter to the other.
Now, you will feel no cold,
for each of you will be warmth to the other.
Now, there is no more loneliness for you,
Now, there is no more loneliness.
Now, you are two bodies, but there is one life before you.
Go now to your dwelling place, to enter into your days of togetherness,
And may your days be good, and long upon the earth.'

Finally the celebrant thanked the four elements and everyone for their presence and for helping to celebrate such a joyous occasion.

After a leisurely stroll back to the coach the jubilant party boarded in readiness for the return journey. Mendelssohn's 'Wedding March' from 'A Midsummer Night's Dream' played as chilled Moet minis were distributed from cold boxes to be drunk through innovative flashing straws. Before the journey ended everyone selected an angel card from a basket that offered individual thoughts for the day.

Drinks:
Back at the couple's home a CD of early morning birdsong played as Bloody Mary and more champagne was served. Carol and Pam showed off their rings each set with their own birthstones. Pam being born in September wore sapphires symbolising serenity and truth. Carol, with a July birthday, had rubies that represented love, enthusiasm and strength.

The Setting:
Pam and Carol's flat was badly in need of redecoration but had been transformed for the occasion with large potted plants hired from a garden centre and skilfully lit, creating the illusion of a sub-tropical paradise.

Refreshments:
Breakfast was laid on a length of fabric the colour of the night sky that twinkled with gold stars and moons. To Carol and Pam's delight their parents arrived in time for the meal. Everyone was encouraged to help themselves from the mouth-watering buffet with the eggs cooked to order:

- Eggs Charlotte, a toasted muffin with smoked salmon and topped with a poached egg and hollandaise sauce.
- Croissants and preserves.
- Enormous bowls of strawberries and raspberries served with clotted cream and a pyramid of ripe, juicy peaches.
- A selection of chilled fruit juices, tea and coffee.

Cushions on the floor were used as additional seating for the meal.

Cake and Speeches:
The cake echoed the theme of the invitations. Iced in dark blue and gold it resulted in everyone's teeth turning blue, which nevertheless offered a hilarious photographic opportunity.

Both Carol and Pam in turn toasted their birth mother and new mother, each replied emotionally to the effect that they were not losing a daughter but gaining one. Pam's father put an arm around both women and hugged them to him, this simple gesture spoke volumes. A friend toasted the couple and explained with a great deal of humour the meaning of Carol and Pam's star signs. The newly banded couple then announced their intention to hyphenate their surnames.

Entertainment:
Guests were asked to sign their names on the freshly decorated bathroom walls for which a bold waterproof pen was provided. Before Pam and Carol departed, party bombs were detonated with a bang, filling the room with brightly coloured metallic symbols of good luck, hearts, black cats, horseshoes and wishbones.

Departure:
Eventually everybody waved Carol and Pam goodbye, laughing at the two helium filled balloons that had been attached to the back of the taxi, each one marked with a bold red letter 'L'.

Notes:
Sometimes it helps to include family members in planning the ceremony to reassure them that it is going to be a beautiful and gracious occasion and that in no way will it embarrass or offend. It may help to emphasise that the ceremony will not mock traditional marriage but is an occasion to celebrate the loving commitment of the couple.

The ceremony was written and conducted by a celebrant trained by Choice Ceremonies.
Tel: 0203 8086 1256
Website: www.choiceceremonies.co.uk

Flashing straws are obtainable from Pink Products.
Website: www.pinkproducts.co.uk

'Morning Birds' Sounds of the earth CD. DDD ORN 5430-2

ANCIENT AND MODERN

A pre-wedding honeymoon was followed by a civil ceremony and church blessing with a reception for twenty. A further celebration took place two weeks later with eighty guests on a river cruise.

As mother of the bridegroom I particularly enjoyed this wonderful wedding as I was free of all responsibility and was able to savour every delicious moment, although I did cater for the river cruise.

Proposal:
Nick asked Janette's father for his daughter's hand in marriage. This followed a romantic proposal during the eclipse while on holiday in France.

Action Plan:
The couple decided on a pre-wedding honeymoon as they planned to marry in June, which would not have been an ideal time of year to visit Thailand due to the climate. As Nick had been married before they decided to adapt a traditional wedding to suit their needs and style; elegant and sincere but with touches of humour.

A jazz river cruise was also arranged to take place two weeks after the wedding for eighty guests. In contrast to the intimate and traditional wedding day, this was to be a wildly colourful party.

Janette and Nick entertained the minister and his wife to dinner. Over the meal they discussed arrangements for their wedding and the contents of the service of blessing.

They also made an appointment with the Superintendent Registrar to organise the civil ceremony.

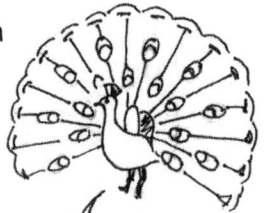

Invitations:

An etching of the picturesque and historic castle where the wedding and reception were to take place decorated the front of the invitations. These were sent to twenty guests who were either family or very close friends of Janette and Nick.

Hen and Stag Party:

What a wonderful excuse for a visit to a health spa! The couple enjoyed a pre-wedding gift of an indulgent day together being pampered from head to toe.

Bridal Wear:

Janette wore a simple but elegant embroidered cream linen dress with a long jacket and matching silk hat. She carried a hand-tied bunch of cream roses, their petals delicately edged with pink.

My catering partner from the sixties, Jenny, who had just retired, agreed to make Janette's bouquet and arrange the flowers for both occasions.

Groom's Wear:

Nick wore a charcoal grey suit that had been made to measure while on holiday in Thailand. He wore a gold rose in his buttonhole that matched his cravat and a colourful brocade waistcoat. His best man dressed in a similar way.

Transport:

The wedding car carrying Janette and her father paused beside the lake where they admired the black swans. The long driveway led to a raised portcullis on which white doves perched. Eventually the car drew to a halt within the high castle walls.

The Setting:

A search for the perfect venue had taken the couple on an enjoyable tour of the countryside. They were immediately attracted to the nine hundred year old castle and its beautiful surroundings, knowing that it would also have romantic associations for them in the future.

We gathered in the drawing room of this resplendent castle where coffee and biscuits were served before moving through to the registered marriage room to await the arrival of the bride.

Civil Ceremony:

Wood panelled walls created a perfect backdrop for the prolific all white flower arrangements containing lilies, lisianthus, stocks, roses and an interesting selection of variegated foliage. Thick white candles were combined within the arrangements that were placed either end of the long tapestry covered table, where the marriage register waited.

106

Two registrars were present. The superintendent registrar's quiet and friendly disposition put everyone at ease as she gave permission for photographs and video recordings to be made throughout the ceremony.

Janette entered the room with her father taking her place beside Nick. The couple declared that they knew no reason why they should not be joined in matrimony and the marriage was sanctioned according to the law, before witnesses. Having made their declarations to one another they were invited by the registrar to kiss. She congratulated them and wished them a long and happy marriage. With the formalities over and the register signed, everyone stepped through the garden door into the bright June sunshine.

The newlyweds strolled hand in hand accompanied by their guests to the picturesque 12th Century church situated just beyond the castle walls. The grey stone font cascaded with fragrant white blooms, blowsy roses, lilies and stocks, as did the pedestal arrangement beside the lectern.

Service of Blessing:
The organ played as the minister, well known to Nick and Janette, led them to the chancel steps. In the informal but sincere service of blessing, the couple pledged their love and loyalty to one another. They held each other's left hand with their rings touching and the minister placed his stole over their joined hands and blessed them. Janette's ring had belonged to her grandmother and had been re-modelled to fit her finger. A longstanding friend of Nick's gave a reading and the minister spoke for a while, adding a light-hearted anecdote here and there. Music was played on the organ as the party left the cool shade of the church emerging into the bright sunlight of a summer's day.

Alongside the church door was an ancient gateway in the castle wall, a short cut leading back into the grounds.

Photography:
Nick's friend Mark, a professional photographer, took full advantage of the many photo opportunities available looking down from the castle walls and in the romantic nooks and crannies within the gardens.

Janette was given a decorated horseshoe that had belonged to her new sister-in-law's horse. This was quickly captured on film. The photographs were later given to Janette and Nick in a decorative album as a wedding gift.

Drinks:
Champagne, Bucks Fizz and canapés were served as we sauntered in the castle's immaculate gardens, enjoying the fragrance of old-fashioned roses and watching the strutting white peacocks with their delicately fanned tails.

107

The Setting:
By lunchtime the marriage room had been transformed into a dining hall. A large oval table was clothed and scattered with fresh rose petals and laid for twenty. It offered the ideal setting for such a special occasion.

Speeches:
The speeches were short but heartfelt. Coffee and petit fours were savoured in the beautiful garden and shared generously with the peacocks.

Departure:
As we departed, the newlyweds waved us farewell before retiring to the bridal suite, complete with four-poster bed and a jacuzzi, which was a surprisingly modern touch!

Some of us met later in the evening at a local pub for a relaxing drink and snack and to review what had been a truly wonderful wedding.

The following day Janette and Nick returned to their cottage where a small group had gathered to enjoy the opening of wedding presents, Janette carefully kept a list of the gifts and their donors. We drank champagne and enjoyed a finger buffet followed by the couple cutting a token wedding cake. Finally, with Bella and Hattie, their two spaniels, they drove towards the west country for a week of reflection and relaxation, their vehicle billowing with balloons,

The River Cruise

Two weeks later Nick and Janette celebrated their marriage with family and a large number of friends on a river cruise. The mood of this occasion was, in contrast to the wedding day, with wildly clashing colours and a jazz band.

Invitations:
Guests received invitations decorated with city landmarks, the embarkation point for the cruise was chosen because of its convenient location near to main line stations and car parks. A train timetable was included together with a diagram showing the route to the pier.

Having combined two homes Janette and Nick needed little in the way of gifts; however, for those who asked, a list of practical items was available.

Dress:
For the party Janette wore a cocktail dress of plum coloured silk, a smart and useful addition to her wardrobe that had been made to measure for her while on holiday in Thailand.

Nick's choice of outfit for a relaxed summer day was a beige linen suit and silk shirt.

The Setting:
The vessel awaited us, the upper deck was open with comfortable seating and the jazz band played on the lower deck where a dance floor encouraged the energetic to perform. Every available corner contained exotic flowers in clashing colours, gerbera, roses, antirrhinums and purple stocks together with lime green chrysanthemums.

Drinks:
The bar was organised and staffed by the crew. Red and white wine, beer and champagne were served with a variety of soft drinks throughout the party.

Refreshments:
We served a selection of hot and cold finger food from the galley. Piles of plates were interleaved with serviettes in orange, red, purple, lime green and shocking pink that linked with the colours of the flowers and cake.

Cake and Speeches:
The wedding cake that had been baked by Janette's mother and iced by me became the focal point of the proceedings. It represented a series of parcels of differing shapes and sizes that were piled one on top of the other. Each parcel was wrapped in brightly coloured fondant icing, adorned with ribbons and scattered with party glitter. The additional small box on top was designed to surprise.

During his speech Nick thanked everyone for helping to celebrate their recent marriage. As a finale to the formalities he lit the topmost box which contained a firework, the cabin was filled with a burst of tiny golden stars and the sounds of oohs and aahs.

Entertainment:
The jazz band played and guests danced as the boat wound its way down river, all on board enjoyed viewing the many famous and interesting landmarks.

Nick's sister, Carrie, had created a collage of childhood photographs of her brother and Janette, which provoked much conversation and laughter.

Departure:
Nick, Janette and a group of friends went out for dinner in the evening.

Gifts:
Among the practical gifts received by the couple were a composter,

wheelbarrow, gardening tools, a kettle and pots and pans for their newly acquired Aga.

Many gifts were given as a surprise, some with a touch of luxury.

Notes:
The starburst referred to can be obtained from most specialist cake decoration shops. We checked with the ship's captain before lighting it.

EASTER PARADE

*A church wedding on Easter Monday was followed
by a reception for fifty guests and an evening party
for eighty.*

The night following my meeting with Charlotte and her mother
in their cosy farmhouse kitchen, I had a dream, which I self-
consciously divulged to them. This resulted in the wedding
adopting a nursery rhyme theme. Charlotte, known to all as
Charlie, and George wanted their special day to be informal, relaxed and expressive of their personalities. George was happy
for Charlie and her Mum to make the arrangements but he
would have his say in the things that mattered to him. Two
definite decisions were made, George was adamant that he
would not wear a tie and Charlie had no intention of wearing
a 'meringue' as this would be totally out of keeping with her
character and lifestyle.

Proposal:
George popped the question to Charlie by text message. His
proposal, which came completely out of the blue, was accepted in the same manner.

Action Plan:
I revisited the bride-to-be and her mother to discuss menus
for the wedding reception and 'walk the course', as it were.
With some imagination we were able to visualise the use of
a collection of ancient outbuildings and a barn as reception areas. With a marquee attached ample space would
be available for the tables to be laid formally and a dance
floor. The marquee hire company skilfully translated our
ideas and supplied all the ancillary items.

Both families attended the Sunday service for three
weeks prior to the wedding to hear the couple's banns
called.

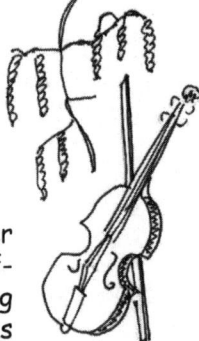

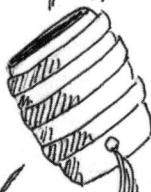

Hen and Stag Parties:

Charlie's girl friends arranged a facial, manicure and pedicure session for her hen night, all of which were somewhat unfamiliar experiences for her. Afterwards they took her out to supper.

The bridegroom's friends, all wearing matching T-shirts decorated with a mug shot of George took him on a pub-crawl through local villages by tractor and trailer. Both parties ended up either by design or coincidence in the same pub!

Invitations:

Invitations announcing the wedding were made by Charlie's Mum and decorated with pressed flowers collected the previous year from their wildflower meadow. The tiny village church had only a limited seating capacity therefore only family and close friends were invited to the wedding and the lunch that followed. Separate invitations were sent to additional guests for the evening party.

The couple decided not to include a gift list with the invitation, preferring to wait until guests asked.

Bridal Wear:

Charlie's ankle-length dress of blue and white striped cotton was finished with a blue sash. She carried a tied bunch of highly scented cream narcissi, blue hyacinths, catkins and pussy willow and wore her fair hair swept back and tied with a blue ribbon. Her choice of dress was a surprise to all who knew her as, being such a tomboy, everyone expected her to dress for her wedding in faded jeans and a baggy sweater.

Groom's Wear:

George and his brother, Steve, who was his best man, wore dark trousers and collarless shirts beneath their cream linen jackets.

Attendants:

Both little bridesmaids wore Bo-Peep style dresses made in pale blue cotton, with laced velvet bodices. Their bonnets were blue and they carried beribboned and decorated crooks. Their outfits would make ideal party wear afterwards.

The three-year-old pageboy was dressed in a cream linen smock and carried a floppy, black toy lamb.

Transport:

Since having her first pony at the age of four, Charlie always dreamed of riding horseback to her wedding, but when the time came her beloved mare was in foal.

The jovial procession left the farmhouse on foot and in spite of the chill air the sun was shining. The narrow lane leading to the church was banked with primroses and a few precious violets hiding beneath the hedgerows. The bells rang out a welcome as Charlie and her Dad walked together, arm in arm, followed by the bridesmaids, the pageboy and other close family members.

Marriage Ceremony:
The Minister, in his Easter vestments of white and gold waited at the church door to welcome the bridal party. Spring flowers filled the church following the Easter Sunday celebration.

With her father, Charlie walked up the aisle to stand beside George who awaited her, as the organist played 'Summer is Comin' In'. Having reached the transept her father kissed his daughter's cheek and stepped back. At Charlie's request he did not give her away as she disliked the concept of being owned. Following the marriage ceremony and the signing of the register, the sacrament of Holy Communion was celebrated. The newlyweds walked arm in arm towards the west door to the strains of an old Cornish air 'The Floral Dance.' The church bells pealed and outside a crowd of well-wishers were gathered.

Photography:
The bridesmaids offered Easter biscuits from a basket to the congregation as they left the church. Charlie and George posed briefly for several formal photographs in the churchyard. Throughout the day informal shots were taken including photos with family pets and farm animals, especially the pregnant mum!

The procession reassembled and a fiddler led the bridal party and their guests back to the farmhouse playing jaunty tunes on the way. Delicate petals from blackthorn flowers fluttered in the breeze providing nature's confetti.

The Setting:
It had been hoped that the bulbs planted either side of the pathway leading to the barn would now be in bloom; unfortunately this was not the case. To introduce instant colour, jam jars full of cut daffodils from the market had been sunk into the earth as a substitute.

Drinks:
A shimmering curtain of agricultural fleece gave a gauzy effect disguising the old dairy. Champagne, wine, local beer from a barrel and Mum's delicious home-made elderflower cordial were among the drinks available. As guests mingled they were invited to request pieces of music to be played by the fiddler.

Speeches:
It was decided that to ease the strain of the day, toasts and speeches would take place before the meal. Glasses of whatever people were drinking were recharged in readiness.

The bride's father asked that everyone join him in a toast to the bride and groom, wishing them long and happy lives together.

The building rang with loud applause and cheers as George began his speech with 'my wife and I'. He thanked Charlie's parents and his own for their help in arranging the wedding and continued by thanking the bridesmaids and pageboy as Charlie gave them each a small token. George thanked everyone for their gifts, adding a few good-humoured jokes about his best man.

Steve had planned his speech carefully cracking a few risqué jokes about Charlie becoming a farmer's wife, including such topics as fertility, foals and some animal jokes. Being a young farmer he could get away with it.

The Setting:
Moving through to the marquee, guests were greeted by a host of golden daffodils, forsythia, catkins, spring greenery and boughs of pussy willow. Large windows stretched the entire length of the marquee offering wonderful views of the tranquil landscape beyond. Even the sheep were there. I stood for a moment looking; it was déjà vu. My dream had come true!

Tables were clothed in dark green linen with gold serviettes, each table having a centrepiece of a small nest containing bright foil-wrapped Easter eggs.

Refreshments:
The meal began with hot chicken broth accompanied by hedgehog rolls and butter. The simplicity of the main course was chosen partly due to limited cooking facilities in the house but mainly because it was a firm family favourite. Sausages and mash with plenty of rich gravy and fresh vegetables were served. Pudding was a meringue nest filled with fruit and cream, each one decorated with a tiny yellow chick.

As the children tired of sitting, they were encouraged to take part in an organised Easter egg hunt with some of the younger adults.

Evening Party:
Following a break, Charlie's sister took responsibility for meeting and greeting additional evening guests, making introductions and ensuring that they all had drinks.

Jugs of fruit punch and Mum's home-made wine were added to the selection on the bar and bales of hay were brought in to provide extra seating before the disco began.

George and Charlie had previously discussed their choice of music with the DJ, giving him a list of requests that were especially important to them. Dancing began with the newlyweds taking the floor as 'All You Need is Love' by the Beatles was played. Delighted, everyone applauded riotously and joined in.

Evening Refreshments:
A ploughman's buffet was set up on trestles covered with hessian and scattered with straw. Farmhouse cheeses, pickles, Scotch eggs, succulent slices of ham and plenty of country style bread and butter were available throughout the evening, to be eaten whenever people were hungry.

Cake:
During a pause in the festivities George and Charlie cut their wedding cake. Made by Charlie's Mum, following an Easter simnel cake recipe it was full of fruit and delicately scented with saffron. The three tiers were covered with a thick layer of marzipan, and as tradition dictates, eleven marzipan balls had been added, one for each disciple excluding Judas.

Departure:
Dancing continued till late. Not wanting to miss a moment of the party Charlie and George stayed to the very end. When eventually they did leave, George must have anticipated that his Land Rover would be an obvious target! So they slipped past it, jumped into an old farm van and drove away.

Gifts:
Many of the couple's gifts were for a modern farming couple, for example an electric bread maker, a wok, an espresso coffee machine and a juicer.

Notes:
The mug shots of George were transferred onto T-shirts using a computer package.

Large umbrellas had been hired in case of showers for the walk to and from church.

Charlie's parents made a generous contribution towards the church flowers.

The decorated marquee was used again later in the week for a fund-raising charity lunch. By arrangement with the company, hire was extended and our china, cutlery and clean table linen were loaned for the occasion. Members of the W.I., of which Charlie's Mother was a part, all contributed towards the meal. A considerable amount of money was raised for a deserving local cause.

HEARTS AND FLOWERS

Twenty-five guests were invited to a garden party and requested to 'dress for Ascot.' The buffet lunch was followed by a surprise.

Michael and Mary's forthcoming marriage was to be kept a secret from their circle of friends until the day of the party. When discussing the catering arrangements with the couple, Michael requested that the day should be a romantic one and as Mary's favourite colour was pink we had a ready made theme with which to work.

Proposal:
The sentimental love song that Michael had written to serenade Mary was also a proposal of marriage following their many years of friendship. Mary accepted his proposal with pleasure.

Action Plan:
Mary and Michael made an appointment with the Superintendent Registrar in the district in which they lived to discuss their wedding arrangements. A notice had to be displayed for fifteen days before a certificate could be issued for their marriage. The notice stated where they intended to marry and was valid for twelve months, they were also asked to produce the following documents:

- A valid passport or birth certificate.
- Proof of address.
- Death certificates of their previous spouses.

Civil Ceremony:
The civil marriage ceremony in which the couple exchanged rings took place at the register office the day before their party. Their grown up children, grandchildren and Michael's two-year-old great grandson attended the occasion. Afterwards they all enjoyed champagne and lunch at a nearby hotel.

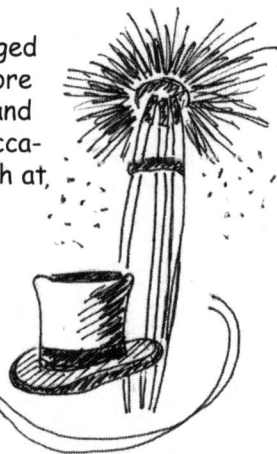

Photography:
The family persuaded Michael and Mary to have a set of studio portraits taken of themselves in their wedding attire.

Invitations:
Michael was renowned for throwing parties of elaborate proportions, often with a theme. On this occasion he telephoned friends inviting them to a garden party, requesting that they dress for Ascot.

Bridal Wear:
Mary decided to wear an Edwardian style dress of dusky pink voile. Her large-brimmed hat of cream straw was vibrant with roses in a range of pinks and reds and she carried a dainty parasol.

Groom's Wear:
Michael wore his morning suit with a top hat; the finishing touch to his ensemble was a red rose in his buttonhole. His trusted companion, Buster, a small wirehaired terrier was constantly at his side, and wore a striking new collar for the occasion.

The Setting:
Michael's spacious bungalow opened onto a sun drenched terrace with formal rose beds and lawns beyond. Garden tables, chairs and large umbrellas offered comfortable seating and shade for guests. Hanging baskets cascaded with seasonal flowers, together with dozens of heart shaped pink balloons that emphasised the theme.

Drinks:
Guests arrived as requested dressed for Ascot and were greeted by Michael and Mary. Pimm's with crackling ice, fruit and sprigs of mint was served with a selection of canapés, which included tiny heart shaped croutons with colourful toppings. When everyone had assembled Michael explained the reason for the party.

Refreshments:
Lunch was a simple but tasteful collation of cold smoked meats and seafood, salads and hot herb bread.

Blessing Ceremony:
Following the meal everyone walked together towards the 13th Century church where their families met them at the lych gate that had been garlanded with flowers in all shades of pink. The service of blessing took place, which included a combination of readings, joyful, traditional and unusual.

On leaving the church the vicar shook hands and congratulated the bride and groom joining them and their guests for a glass of pink champagne that (by prior arrangement) we served in the church porch. At this point Michael, the romantic, produced from behind his back a bouquet of roses in shades of pink and red, a perfect match to those on Mary's hat. He was congratulated on his attention to detail but admitted to having had a tip from Mary's daughter. The party strolled back through the village, this time accompanied by their family, friends and the vicar.

A welcome awaited them in the form of a chimney sweep with a black cat on his shoulder; he congratulated Mary and Michael on their marriage, shook hands and planted a sooty kiss on Mary's cheek. This is an old English custom that is said to bring good luck.

Refreshments:
Lace clothed tables were scattered with rose petals and heart shaped glitter that twinkled in the sunlight as more pink fizz and a selection of teas were served. Everything at this tea party was pink or heart shaped and very dainty:

- Sandwiches with tasty savoury fillings.
- Tiny buttered scones.
- Selections of pretty cakes and fruit tartlets.

Cake and Speeches:
As a surprise, Mary's daughter had organised a cake that was a copy of her mother's hat, with royal icing replicating the straw and handmade sugar paste roses together with a pink ribbon. Champagne toasts and short speeches accompanied the cake cutting.

Entertainment:
During the late afternoon when the young people had departed, some guests chose to relax in the gentle sunshine; the more energetic played croquet and clock golf on the lawn while others enjoyed a few rubbers of bridge. As dusk fell they moved indoors.

Gifts:
The subject of wedding presents was raised, Mary and Michael with two homes to amalgamate needed very little. One guest suggested that they all pledge a promise to the couple and although much laughter ensued the idea proved extremely popular. A few of the more publishable pledges are listed below.

- A pastel portrait of little dog Buster
- Decorating a room.
- Pruning the roses.
- Holiday dog sitting for Buster.

- Four litres of home-made chocolate ice cream, especially for Michael.
- Trimming the front hedge.
- Donating and planting a special tree to commemorate the occasion.

Notes:

An audio recording of the church service was made with the permission of the vicar.

Trees to Celebrate Special Events, International Tree Foundation.

Tel: 01342 712536
E-mail: hq.itf@tree-foundation.org.uk
Website: www.tree-foundation.org.uk

From the roses in the bouquet that Michael had given her, Mary made a quantity of potpourri that she enlivened with perfumed oil.

VIVA LAS VEGAS

An Egyptian-themed wedding in Las Vegas was followed by a Caribbean honeymoon and, in close succession, a UK party.

When I heard that my niece intended to marry in Las Vegas, wild horses wouldn't have kept me away. Debbie and Matt's relationship had developed rather untraditionally. They met, had a baby, bought a house together, then organised the wedding. Determined to do it their way, their big day was again untraditional as they planned an Egyptian-themed wedding in Las Vegas with a handful of their closest relatives flying out for the occasion.

With the wedding plans in place Debbie realised that she was after all a traditionalist at heart and yearned for a formal proposal of marriage from Matt before they left for the United States.

Proposal:
Out of the blue Matt telephoned Debbie and asked her to get ready as they were going out for a posh meal, leaving their son, Sam, in the care of his grandmother. Matt appeared to be in a great hurry to get somewhere before dusk. Debbie thought the restaurant must be a charming building and that he wanted her to see it before dark. They drove into the sunset, eventually stopping at a beauty spot renowned for its fabulous views. Matt went to the boot of the car and produced two bags plus a sheet of instructions, which read 'close your eyes, count slowly to fifty, then undo the first bag and put on the clothes'. 'Undo the second bag, take the items and sit by the tree and wait'. Matt disappeared. Debbie obediently followed the instructions. In the first bag she found a beautiful scarlet medieval dress, complete with headdress. In the second was a tartan rug. Giggling, she dressed and as requested sat on the rug and waited. Matt appeared in full armour. Getting down on

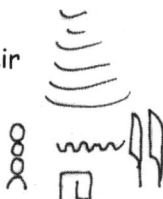

one knee, he asked her to marry him. Debbie replied, "yes, yes, of course". The proposal was followed by dinner at a castle.

Action Plan:
Matt and Debbie made all necessary reservations for the wedding and honeymoon on the internet. This included:

- Air tickets.
- Wedding venue.
- Hotel accommodation.
- Honeymoon.

In the state of Nevada, USA, it is possible to arrange a wedding in a matter of hours. Currently the requirements are the provision of birth certificates, photographs and passports for identification. Knowing that many American states require a blood test, the couple checked but this was not necessary in Nevada.

For their honeymoon Matt and Debbie would have preferred an opportunity to discover the secrets of ancient Egypt as they cruised down the Nile but a beach holiday seemed more appropriate for fourteen-month old Sam.

Detailed arrangements were e-mailed to the wedding guests.

- The estimated time of arrival of the wedding party and other guests.
- A list of hotels where guests would be staying, with addresses and contact numbers.
- An indication of where the group planned to meet for meals.
- A timetable of events for the wedding day.

They also arranged an Egyptian-themed party to take place on their return to the UK.

Invitations:
Handcrafted invitations to the UK party were designed and made by Debbie, offering a personal touch that could not be equalled. They took the shape of scrolls and were decorated with hieroglyphics and tied with a silver cord.

A gift list was available. Details were sent separately if requested.

Hen and Stag Parties:
Having arrived in Vegas two days prior to the wedding, we all met for dinner at the designated hotel. Debbie's Mum volunteered to care for Sam, while the remainder of the women visited the hotel's Oasis Spa. Here healing hands and soothing elixirs provided a unique haven for relaxation.

The men visited a sizzling and provocative dance revue and later hit the casinos.

Bridal Wear:
For her wedding Debbie wore a silk chemise with matching trousers of misty sea blue with silver trimmings and Egyptian jewellery. Her hair was piled high on which she wore a diamond tiara. Kohl-rimmed eyes, crystal-studded brows and her hands and feet decorated with henna were additional complementary touches to her appearance.

Groom's Wear:
Matt's chemise of sand-coloured linen was worn over a cream shirt with baggy trousers. His flamboyant Egyptian headdress in blue and silver lamé continued the dramatic theme.

The Setting:
As we waited at the Vegas Wedding Chapel an Elvis look-a-like wearing a sparkling gold jacket escorted the previous wedding party to their waiting limo. Within a short while the Elvis scene was transformed into an Egyptian theme. The spacious room was decorated with a sarcophagus, Egyptian paintings, golden sphinx and drapes with swags and tassels. An atmospheric mist filled the chapel as we entered creating a feeling of timelessness and anticipation.

Marriage Ceremony:
Standing on a plinth Matt awaited Debbie's arrival. We watched as he was entertained by a belly dancer whose scantily clad body gyrated before him.

Eyes turned as Debbie made her dramatic entrance, carried on Cleopatra's golden throne by two barefooted, muscle bound slaves wearing only loincloths.

As we looked on King Tutankhamun married the couple in a short but dramatic ceremony in which Matt and Debbie read from scrolls the words they had written themselves. Their promises included care for their son, Sam, who slept peacefully in his pushchair throughout the ceremony. King Tutankhamun spoke about the wedding rings being a symbol of unity into which lives are joined in an unbroken circle.

From a side office the registrar, who had witnessed the ceremony, pronounced Matt and Debbie man and wife in the eyes of the law. It was then that the couple signed the marriage register.

Photography:
The newlyweds returned to the plinth where they posed for official photographs, being first joined by Sam and their parents and then by other relatives.

The marriage ceremony was transmitted over the internet to the UK where those unable to attend the wedding were able to watch it live, albeit at 2 am! The web link was available for three months after the wedding and became an integral part of their UK party.

Instead of being given a lucky black cat or horseshoe, as is the custom in England, Debbie received a carved wooden camel as a token of good fortune, which continued the Egyptian theme.

One of the wedding guests made contact with an elderly relative in England by mobile phone, as they wanted to be one of the first to con-gratulate Debbie and Matt on their marriage.

It was twilight as King Tutankhamun walked the newly married couple to their white stretch limousine. Sam was lifted aboard in his pushchair amongst a cloud of bubbles blown by Debbie's niece, Aimee. Meanwhile the overhead neon lights flashed dramatically illustrating the message 'Congratulations on your wedding day, Debbie and Matt.'

The Setting:
We drove slowly down the famous Strip, lined with themed hotels, dazed by the razzmatazz and multi-coloured flashing neon lights. Eventually approaching the vast pyramid-shaped hotel where Debbie, Matt and Sam were staying. The Luxor was adorned inside and out in true Egyptian style overlooked by a statue of King Tutankhamun and the golden sphinx. It was full of night clubs, restaurants, an Imax theatre, museum and floor upon floor of luxury accommodation.

Drinks:
We gathered in the hotel foyer for drinks where haunting, echoing music played as we watched a caricaturist capture an incredible likeness of Matt and Debbie in their exotic wedding attire.

Entertainment:
To work up a good appetite the entire party set out for a walk down The Strip with Sam, now wide awake, in his pushchair decorated with balloons.

Absorbing the non-stop party atmosphere of one of the cities that sel-dom sleeps was an unforgettable experience full of glamour, entertain-ment, music and gaiety.

Refreshments:
With so many choices it was difficult to decide where to dine. Eventually we all agreed to return to The Luxor. Passing through hall after hall

of casinos we eventually arrived at Pharaoh's Pheast Buffet, which featured a thirty-foot salad bar, two carvery stations and specialities from around the world. A vast selection of desserts was available including the tantalizing Rugalach Cheesecake.

Gifts:
The majority of gifts received by Matt and Debbie were wonderfully practical but one touch of originality was a garland created from a collection of wedding memorabilia, which included the wooden camel, champagne corks, Debbie's bangles and tiara.

Notes:
Debbie's sister and her two small children, who were unable to make the journey to Las Vegas, watched the web link next day with some friends. Debbie had thoughtfully put together a surprise goodie bag for her which contained:

Bottle of champagne.
Large box of chocolates.
Balloons, blowers and streamers.
Disposable camera.
An album for her photographs.
A lottery ticket.

Vegas Wedding Chapel.
Website: www.vivalasvegasweddings.com

Garlands of Memorabilia, because of their fragility hand delivery/collection is necessary, which restricts the service to the south of England. For brochure:
Tel: 01403 273754

HORN OF PLENTY

*An Evangelical Church ceremony
and a reception with the congregation taking part.*

Richard and Jane had both been through difficult times but eventually found solace in worshipping at the same church. Jane, a Sunday school teacher met Richard who was involved with the Boys' Brigade. It was important to them both to be able to celebrate their special day with the people who had become their friends.

Action Plan:
Following the announcement of their engagement members of the church congregation were anxious to be involved with the wedding and help in any way they could.

Prior to the wedding Richard and Jane attended several preparation sessions with the minister. These sessions covered such areas as the Christian understanding of marriage, a detailed exploration of the meaning and implications of the vows and promises, and the content of the service itself. A rehearsal was also arranged at a convenient time prior to the wedding day.

Invitations:
Jane and Richard asked the minister to make an announcement in church inviting everybody to the wedding and to join them afterwards in the church hall for light refreshments. The invitation was also included in the church newsletter with a note that read: 'Please do not bring gifts, just yourselves'.

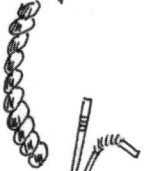

Hen and Stag Parties:
Jane was invited to a friend's house where many of the ladies from the church provided a buffet lunch in her honour. Everyone brought a copy of a favourite poem or a recipe that was later collated into a book and given to her.

Richard spent an evening dining with his best man and a group of friends.

Bridal Wear:
For the wedding Jane hired the dress of her dreams, made in delicate white lace over satin, the floor-length gown fell into a short train. Instead of a bouquet she carried a white bible with a silk bookmark that was decorated with a single red rose.

Groom's Wear:
Richard and his best man wore lounge suits with a red rose in their buttonholes.

Photography:
Photographs had not been high on the couple's list of priorities but cameras flashed from every angle. They received many copies over the months following the wedding, all of which found a place in their treasured album.

Transport:
The owner of an Austin Seven wore many hats that day. Having valeted the interior and attached the white ribbons he drove Jane to church. Furthermore he deemed it a privilege to be the one to escort her up the aisle to join her husband-to-be and 'give her away.'

Marriage Ceremony:
A wonderful display of seasonal flowers had been arranged by ladies taking their turn on the church flower rota. The blooms were colour-coordinated with a wedding that took place earlier in the day, which meant that the two brides were able to share the cost of the flowers.

Jane entered the church on the arm of her chauffeur and friend to 'Be Still' composed by David J Evans. The marriage service was the focus of the day with friends taking part and it began with words of welcome from the Minister.

- Hymn: 'Praise my Soul the King of Heaven.'
- A youth pastor spoke about the Christian viewpoint of marriage.
- The Lord's Prayer.
- Readings from the New Testament.
- A solo was sung by friend, Annie, with Kay on clarinet and Suzie on piano.
- Hymn: 'The King of Love My Shepherd Is.'
- Reflections.
- The Marriage Covenant, during which the couple faced one another as they made their vows. The rings had been made by Richard in an evening class and were engraved with their initials and the date of the wedding.
- Prayers.
- Hymn: 'How Sweet the Name of Jesus Sounds'.

- Holy Communion: Prayer of Thanksgiving, Words of Institution, Sharing the Bread and the Cup, Prayer of Commitment.
- Hymn: 'Love Divine all Loves Excelling' during which Richard and Jane signed the marriage register.

Two small girls walked before the newlyweds scattering rose petals as they walked down the aisle. The Sunday school children followed, dancing and shaking their tambourines, singing 'Shine Jesus Shine.'

As the newly married couple stepped outside into the gentle sunshine they were met with a surprise. During the signing of the register the Boys' Brigade band had positioned themselves forming a guard of honour. On trumpet, cornet, penny whistles, drums and bugles they played 'Love and Marriage' in celebration of the occasion. Rice was thrown as many cameras clicked capturing the sublimely happy moment.

The Setting:
The adjoining church hall was set ready for the reception. A few small tables and chairs were available for those who could not stand for too long. Younger guests were encouraged to circulate. The church flower arrangers had generously extended their skills to include beautiful posies for the tables.

Drinks:
Due to the couple's personal preference a soft drinks bar was provided. Iced tea and coffee, fruit juices and milkshakes in many different flavours were available.

Refreshments:
Jane and Richard received numerous offers of help towards the refreshments. They were grateful for such kindness but aware that, without organisation, the catering could become chaotic. Charts were produced of interesting finger food, together with an estimate of the number of items required. Friends ticked as many boxes as they chose, depending on what they were prepared to provide, using Fair Trade items available through the Church wherever possible. Richard and Jane were responsible for the final shopping spree.

A small group of friends arranged the finger food in neat rows on doilyed trays, garnishing them with fresh flower heads.

The Minister said a short Grace. Then the older children handed round the trays of delicious and attractively displayed food, of both sweet and savoury combinations.

Cake and Speeches:
While Richard was occupied making the wedding rings, Jane attended a

cake decoration course. The design she chose for their wedding cake was an open book; on one page she piped their names and the wedding date, on the other a cluster of delicate, handmade red sugar roses.

Richard gave a short but sincere speech of thanks to everyone present, proposing a toast to 'love and friendship'.

The best man asked that glasses be raised for the second time to drink a toast to 'Jane and Richard'. Their names were echoed as glasses of sparkling elderflower cordial toasted the future happiness of the couple. The cake cutting followed.

Entertainment:
There was yet another surprise for almost everyone when the Sunday school children gathered to sing. Several rehearsals had taken place in secret and Jane was overwhelmed, in fact tearful with joy at the children's performance.

During the reception, guests were invited to sign a linen tablecloth that would later be embroidered and given to the couple as a memento of their special day.

Departure:
More rice was thrown as the pair left for a romantic city break. The Austin Seven again revved into action, accompanied by a strong smell of kippers toasting on the exhaust. Richard's friends had revived this old custom.

YULETIDE

*A candlelight wedding and reception with a Christmas
theme for one hundred and fifty guests,
who were entertained by mummers.*

With barely six months to organise their wedding, Geoff and
Frances entrusted me with many of the practical arrangements
and seasonal touches. Having discussed their ideas and budget
they felt free to concentrate on their personal preparations
leaving me to co-ordinate the remainder.

Action Plan:
In June Geoff learned that his company contract was to take
him abroad early in the New Year. He and Frances decided to
take advantage of the season and plan their wedding around
the festive warmth and tradition of Christmas.

The couple discussed arrangements for their wedding with
the priest, who to save time, e-mailed details of the service
to and fro until the content was agreed.

Having confirmed the date of the wedding, Frances sent a note
to the principal guests asking them to keep it free.

Invitations:
Choosing the stationery was an important and personal priority
for the bride. She ordered a matching set of invitations, order
of service sheets, menus, cake boxes, place and thank you
cards, all of which echoed the festive theme. Bright red and
green, holly-shaped confetti was added to each envelope,
with a note informing guests that their gift list was lodged with
a well-known department store.

Hen and Stag Parties:
Although time was at a premium, Frances was delighted to be
invited by her friends to a West End show with her mother
and sister included.

The best man organised a parachute jump for Geoff and a group of friends to take place in the New Year. This allowed time for the participants to find sponsors in order to raise funds for the charity with which Geoff was involved.

Bridal Wear:
For her wedding Frances wore a bias-cut dress with ruffled bodice, long sleeves and a train. The pale gold velvet was decorated with clusters of tiny diamanté motifs that matched her tiara and shimmered in the candlelight.

The warmth of the season was reflected in her bouquet of rich dark red roses, amaryllis, fragrant white stephanotis and touches of gold.

Groom's Wear:
Geoff, his best man and ushers wore extravagantly embroidered red and gold silk waistcoats and matching cravats with their frock coats, each with a rose in his buttonhole.

Attendants:
Twins, Simon and Matthew, were pageboys, or best boys, as they preferred to be called and wore the military uniform of drummer boys and carried toy drums.

Photography:
Having booked a photographer the idea was extended to include a video. Copies were sent as Christmas presents to close family and to those unable to attend the wedding.

Marriage Ceremony:
It was a grey December day but the bells were ringing merrily as guests gathered in the church. An array of gilded fruits, cones and holly together with gold and burgundy blooms created a festive display. Each sill and ledge twinkled with tiny star-shaped candles.

The priest led the procession of choristers who carried glowing lanterns. Frances accompanied by her father followed and finally the two drummer boys brought up the rear. They moved sedately towards the sanctuary steps where Geoff waited as the organist played 'Pastoral' from the eighth concerto by Corelli. The service was interwoven with advent carols, hymns, prayers and readings. During the signing of the marriage register a choirboy sang 'Walking In the Air' from 'The Snowman' by Howard Blake. On leaving the vestry a lighted gold candle complemented Frances' bouquet, which provided a magical glow. As she walked down the aisle beside her new husband, the choir sang 'Noel of the Birds' accompanied by the organ.

Transport:
Geoff's brother, the proud owner of a white classic Rover Sixty, thankfully with a heater, offered the car and his services as chauffeur for the day. There was a bottle of champagne and two glasses ready for the newlyweds to have a quiet drink together on their way to the reception.

The Setting:
On arrival at the bride's family home, guests were greeted at the cottage door with a visual and sensual welcome. Imitation snow covered the roof of the porch, surrounding shrubs and sprinkled the festive garland that hung on the heavy oak door. A spicy aroma filled the air achieved by burning incense and wine mulling in the nearby kitchen.

Guests made their way through the hallway into the welcoming warmth of the drawing room and on to the carpeted walkway that led to the marquee. Drinks and cocktail savouries were served as they waited to be received by the wedding party.

The ceiling of the marquee was lined in black to produce the effect of a night sky with a myriad of twinkling stars. A large Christmas tree decorated with coloured lights stood near the entrance under which gifts were placed.

Circular tables each seating ten were covered with rich burgundy cloths and sprinkled with tiny golden stars. Linen napkins tied like a parcel with ribbon and a name label marked each place setting. Miniature Christmas trees in gold pots decorated the tables and were highlighted by narrow beams of light centred over every table providing a sparkling and intimate atmosphere for the diners.

Drinks:
Christmas music played as the newly married couple welcomed their guests standing beneath a large bunch of mistletoe. A choice of champagne, hot mulled red wine or non-alcoholic cranberry sparkle, made with equal parts cranberry juice, apple juice and ginger ale were offered from trays scattered with sparkly gold confetti. Spiced nuts, tiny star-shaped sandwiches, honey-baked sausages, stuffed bacon rolls and fingers of brie wrapped in filo pastry were served hot with a cranberry dip and offered in substantial amounts to double as a starter.

Cake and Speeches:
Glasses were refilled and the guests seated us attention was drawn to the cake cutting and speeches, the formalities were held before the meal enabling the speechmakers to relax.

A stone garden pedestal in the centre of the marquee provided a sophisticated stand for the wedding cake. The two lower tiers were placed one on top of the other with the third supported by tall pillars and crowned with three lighted golden candles of varying heights. Sprigs of holly and variegated ivy delicately crafted in sugar entwined the tiers.

The bride's father proposed a toast to "Frances and Geoff".

The groom in his speech mentioned his stag night challenge, grasping the opportunity to drum up some sponsorship for the parachute jump.

Announcing that the bride and groom were about to cut the cake, the best man explained the symbolism behind this tradition as being the couple's first action together as man and wife. The sharing out of cake that takes place later binds guests together and sending pieces to absent friends shows that their presence was missed.

Refreshments:
During the meal the brass band seated on a dias played a great mix of music from classical pieces to popular tunes from musicals and films.

Diners enjoyed a traditional Christmas meal of roast turkey with all the trimmings, followed by iced Christmas pudding and star-shaped short-breads. Fingers of assorted cheeses with grapes were served, followed by coffee, wedding cake and miniature mince pies.

Entertainment:
When the children had finished eating, they were given paper and felt-tip pens and asked to draw a picture of Frances and Geoff on their wedding day. Each child signed their drawing; these were later framed and now hang in the couple's hallway.

The best man announced the arrival of The Mummers. He explained that traditionally ancient folk dramas were performed mainly at Christmas time, this being a means by which the poor obtained charity from the rich. He introduced the players as follows:

- St. George, the hero.
- Two bad Turkish knights.
- The village rascal, with rag dolls attached to his person, representing his many children.
- The doctor/medicine man, with his magic potions.
- Father Christmas who pleaded throughout for plum pudding, mince pies and a pot of good ale.

The plot slowly revealed itself and a bloody fight took place between the hero and the Turkish knights. As St. George lay dying a frantic call is sent out for the Doctor who comes and heals the expiring hero with magic potions. The dark figures steal away and the hero rises triumphantly.

134

Following the drama, players were duly plied with hot mince pies and a 'pot of good ale'.

The lights dimmed and the band began by playing Le Roy Anderson's 'Christmas Festival'. The concert continued with The Mummers leading the singing of carols and everybody joined in.

Departure:
As Frances and Geoff prepared to leave, Geoff enveloped his wife in a warm burgundy cloak trimmed with white fur. Flaming torches lined the driveway as guests gathered with lighted sparklers to wave a dramatic farewell to the newly married couple. As their car reached the end of the driveway cascades of dancing, colourful and noisy fireworks filled the sky.

Gifts:
One of the couple's wedding gifts was a Methuselah of champagne, to be used for their house warming party.

Notes:
Special care was taken when choosing the heating system for the marquee, as the comfort of guests depended on this being effective. We worked from the small cottage kitchen and a service tent with Calor gas cookers, hot cupboard, water boilers and the loyal hosepipe. The marquee company also provided mobile toilets.

Ideas for Geoff's stag night were found on a website.
Website: www.confetti.co.ukhen_stag.asp

Fireworks, torches and sparklers can be ordered from Millennium Fireworks.
Tel: 01884 840504
Fax: 01884841142

The snow machine was hired from Theme Traders.
Tel: 020 8452 8518
Website: www.themetraders.com

SUMMER GARDEN

A civil marriage was followed by an Interfaith ceremony beneath a willow tree, continuing with a finger buffet for fifty guests and a river departure.

Dawn and Martin met while working on a river conservation project. They soon discovered that they shared a deep interest in nature and the environment. Arrangements for their wedding were interwoven with as many natural elements as possible.

Proposal:
Martin, ever the romantic, traced the words: 'Will you marry me' into the muddy riverbank with a stick. After having teased him for a while, Dawn traced her reply, which was: 'Yes I will.'

Action Plan:
The couple felt deeply disappointed when they realised that, as Martin was divorced, the local vicar would not marry them in church. As an alternative he offered a service of blessing that could follow a civil marriage. Dawn felt rejected especially as she had been baptised and confirmed in the church. Her family had lived and taken part in village life for over three hundred years and many of her ancestors lay at rest in the graveyard.

A friend introduced them to an Interfaith Minister whom they realised could create a spiritual service especially for them. They discovered that the ceremony could be personally meaningful and totally sincere, illuminating their own values and beliefs while giving expression to their personalities.

To legalise their marriage Martin and Dawn booked a civil ceremony at their local register office to take place prior to their Interfaith wedding.

Invitations:
Making the invitations was not only a cost-saving exercise but also an enjoyable project between Dawn and her young niece. Using handmade paper into

which tiny petals had been compressed, they wrote the date, time and place of the wedding. A packet of flower seeds of the variety that attract butterflies and insects was attached before being sealed into bright lime-green envelopes.

Hen and Stag Parties:
Dawn was invited to dinner at her sister's home where she met twelve friends who had been invited as a surprise and who showered her with gifts. The presents they brought were connected with her interest in the conservation of wildlife and were as follows:

- Bat box
- Bird feeders
- Nesting boxes
- Ladybird house
- Toad pot

Several weeks before the wedding Martin and some of his closest friends took a trip to France. This was partly an excuse to have fun but also an opportunity to purchase champagne and wines for the wedding.

Civil Ceremony
Martin and Dawn made a low-key visit to the register office with two witnesses, to complete the formalities of a civil marriage and provide the legal documents. They kept the rings to be exchanged during their garden ceremony.

Bridal Wear:
For her wedding Dawn wore an ankle-length dress of Nottingham lace over cream satin which had been designed and made by her mother for her own wedding a quarter of a century before. The only addition was a tiny silver horseshoe from her parents' wedding cake stitched into the hem for good luck.

The hand-tied bunch included delicate lime green alchemilla, mixed garden flowers and purple and white buddleia to attract the butterflies and was secured with natural raffia.

Groom's Wear:
Martin and his best man, Danny, wore navy suits with cream shirts. Their lime green ties carried through the colour theme.

Attendants:
Dawn's sister was maid of honour. She and her young daughter, who was bridesmaid, both wore dresses of lime green raw silk and carried posies of mixed garden flowers. They had tiny butterfly clips in their hair.

Photography:
Martin commissioned a videographer to capture the occasion the resulting film becoming a treasured keepsake. The most intimate moments were played in slow motion. The immaculate garden offered a perfect setting for the photographs that friends took throughout the afternoon with the promise that they would send copies.

The Setting:
Dawn's uncle and aunt offered their garden for the ceremony and reception, with beautifully maintained flowerbeds and lawns that swept down to the river.

The marquee company fitted an awning with open sides that allowed a view of the garden, river and most importantly the willow tree under which Dawn and Martin would make their vows to one other.

The elegant stone statue of a nude female that stood beside the pond, wore a crown of tiny crab apples and fresh flowers.

Drinks:
Music drifted through the garden as guests arrived. Drinks were served from the summerhouse and included a selection of wines and champagne, fruit juices or iced tea and coffee. Large stone jardinières filled with ice were used to cool the bottles.

Marriage Ceremony:
The spiritual ceremony that had been created by Dawn, Martin and the Interfaith Minister took place beneath the willow tree, its overhanging branches forming the roof of their beautiful, outdoor temple, as wind chimes played softly in the breeze.

The ceremony focused on the love, commitment and mutual respect offered by the partners to one another and was interwoven with allusions to nature.

Before making their vows and exchanging rings surrounded by their families and friends, Dawn and Martin placed a garland round each other's neck that they had made themselves from dried grasses, fresh wild flowers and tiny crab apples. The Minister spoke of planting seeds of happiness on this wonderful day, the tender nurturing, one for the other, that would enable their love to blossom and the fruits of a relationship be reaped as they walked through life together.

A pair of caged doves became a focal point. Guests watched as the couple pulled the ribbons that were attached to the cage thus releasing the birds, this being a Filipino tradition symbolising the start of the couple's new lives.

The following words were spoken by the minister:

"May you be blessed with the nourishment of the earth
May you tend each other with the water of compassion, understand-
ing and forgiveness,
And may the fire of love burn forever within your hearts
As you soar together upon the wings of eternity."

Following the ceremony guests were invited to sign a special book to commemorate the occasion and the musicians began to play a jazzed up version
of 'All Things Bright and Beautiful.'

Refreshments:
Champagne flowed. Guests congratulated and toasted the couple as the
string quartet continued to play from the gazebo. People sat wherever
they chose, on garden benches, chairs and patio steps or on picnic rugs
beside the river.

An imaginative selection of vegetarian finger food was handed around from
the buffet, which included:

- A selection of canapés.
- Cheese straws.
- Savoury éclairs.
- Cream cheese and asparagus roulades.
- Vol-au-vent filled with mushrooms and served hot.
- A selection of dips with vegetable crudités.
- Egg and cress sandwiches.
- Tiny savoury quiche, served hot.

For the sweet-toothed a chocolate fountain was in full flow with litres of
luscious white chocolate cascading down the sides. Set on an attractively
laid table it was surrounded by baby doughnuts, fresh strawberries, al-
mond macaroons, marshmallows and more, all piled on to platters ready to
be dipped with the aid of cocktail sticks and plenty of serviettes.

Tea and coffee followed.

The informality of the occasion gave the newlyweds ample opportunity to
spend time with their guests. The little bridesmaid gave each lady a favour,
a dainty lime green package containing five sugared almonds symbolising
health, wealth, happiness, prosperity and fertility. The favours were tied
with a fine ribbon and finished with a tiny butterfly. They had been chosen
with care knowing that it is the small details that are remembered.

Cake and Speeches:
The wedding cake was displayed on a stone pedestal on the patio. Made by
Martin's aunt, each of the three tiers was of a different kind, fruit, lemon

and carrot cake. It was professionally iced and dusted with edible glitter that sparkled in the sunlight. The delicate variegated ivy, tiny flowers and butterflies crafted in sugar looked natural in the garden setting.

Speaking also on behalf of his wife, Dawn's father mentioned his own happy marriage and the joy that having two beautiful daughters and a grand-daughter had brought into their lives. He asked that glasses be raised to drink a toast to the ultimate happiness of Dawn and Martin. In his speech Martin acknowledged his father-in-law's kind words. He thanked the celebrant, their families and friends for making the day so memorable. He continued by reading aloud a love letter he had written to Dawn that was heavily punctuated with humour.

Danny congratulated the bride and her attendants on their amazing appearance. Having attended school with Martin there were many amusing tales to tell! Finally he proposed a toast to the couple and announced the cutting of the wedding cake.

Departure:
As dusk was falling the newlyweds, still in their wedding attire, ran hand in hand towards the end of the garden where a punt awaited their departure. They left in a shower of rose petals then poled at a leisurely pace down river.

Gifts:
A dovecot and garden bench were among the couple's wedding presents.

Notes:
The ceremony was created and conducted by Revd. Jacqueline Clark, Interfaith Minister.
Contact The Interfaith Seminary.
E-mail: admin@thefaithseminary.com
Website: www.theinterfaithseminary.com

The handler delivered the doves at the agreed time and place. Following the release of the birds he collected the cage before returning to base.
The White Dove Company.
Tel: 020 8508 1414
Website: www.thewhitedovecompany.co.uk

Information regarding hire of the chocolate fountain and a choice of flavours which range between milk, dark or white chocolate cappuccino, caramel, strawberry, orange, kiwi and lime.
Tel: 020 8452 8518
Website: www.themetraders.com

As a thank you, Richard and Dawn gave their parents tickets for the theatre. Tickets were also given to the aunt and uncle whose garden they used for the wedding.

All empty bottles were re-cycled.

MUSIC MAKERS

*Musicians gathered for a classical concert.
In the interlude a marriage of hearts took place
that was followed by a wedding breakfast, music
and dancing.*

My invitation to this wonderful wedding came out of the blue. I was invited to become a travelling companion to a friend whose husband was unable to make the journey. Chrissy and Vox, both Smart car owners met on the internet through the Smart Car Club.

Action Plan:

Chrissy, a talented musician herself with many musical friends and connections introduced Vox to her scene. Previously he had taught himself to play a number of instruments and developed a love for all kinds of music, but this was his introduction to a world full of classical musicians. It was around their mutual interests that the wedding was arranged.

Invitations:

The invitations were made by Chrissy using cream deckle-edged cards, which she decorated with two entwined golden rings. The couple were clear that they wanted a lifetime commitment to one other, but Vox had only recently divorced. Guests were invited to help celebrate the union of Vox and Chrissy with a note that read; 'this occasion may precede or follow our civil marriage depending on unpredictable variables. The day will include an exchange of vows, music, a wedding breakfast and dancing'. Guests were invited to bring sleeping bags and tents in order to stay overnight and the musicians among them were asked to bring their instruments.

Bridal Wear:

Chrissy wore a full-length dress of cream crepe with an organza overlay, scoop neckline and

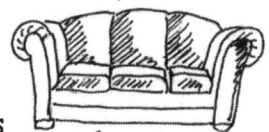

short sleeves. The bodice was laced at the back finishing with a cluster of roses at the waist created from the same fabric.

Groom's Wear:
Vox was dressed in a light grey suit, cream shirt and grey silk tie.

The Setting:
The flint walls of the old farm buildings supported tangles of scented roses, honeysuckle, lavender and clematis and provided shelter for the lawns. The farmhouse and associated cottages were situated around a central courtyard, together with an ancient barn where music is played throughout the warmer months of the year.

Washing facilities and chemical toilets were located in a nearby building for the use of the campers.

Photography:
Several guests had been asked to bring cameras, take lots of photos and send copies as souvenirs of the day. However, a surprise for Vox and Chrissy was the discovery that the caterers had brought extra friends to help. One just happened to be a professional photographer. He presented the couple with a disc containing over 200 images.

Drinks:
Tall glasses of Pimm's and soft drinks were served from beneath a tented awning on the lawn as guests drifted in carrying various instruments to join the celebrations. Chrissy and Vox laughed with their friends as from the wide open doors of one of the barns, music from a grand piano and violin drifted around the garden.

The Setting:
The yard bell sounded and the musicians were asked to assemble in the main barn. The non-playing guests climbed a flight of wooden stairs leading to a hayloft and settled into comfortable sofas and armchairs that echoed the fashion of bygone eras. Down below, the musicians who had travelled from near and far took their places around the conductor who stood on a podium. A violinist played 'Here comes the Bride' as the happy couple walked arm in arm into the company of their friends to riotous applause and wolf whistles. Chrissy and Vox sat side by side on a settee to enjoy the afternoon concert. As the orchestra began to play the old beams rang with Beethoven's 'Pastoral Symphony.'

Ceremony
Following the performance, Chrissy and Vox stood on the podium where a marriage of two hearts took place witnessed by all present. Looking deeply into each other's eyes they spoke of their love for one another.

Tears of emotion were mopped, before two friends, a mother and daughter, sang 'The Flower Song' a duet from the opera 'Lakme' by Delibes. When the applause had died down everyone returned to the garden where, after a short while the heavy metal bell in the yard rang again, this time to signal the wedding breakfast.

Refreshments:
Rows of attractively laid tables were set beneath the ancient beams in yet another barn that had been converted from an old dairy and included a well equipped kitchen.

Regular visitors to the venue were clearly familiar with the routine as the service and collection of food took place in an incredibly organised manner.

A card on each table gave the following instructions:

'Please ensure that a representative from every table is responsible for allocating the following tasks'.

- Make sure that guests unfamiliar with the venue understand the arrangements, know where things are and are comfortable.
- Collect food and serve people on your table.
- Collect more wine/beer/soft drinks when required.
- Make coffee and tea.
- Ensure that the tables are left completely clear at the end of the meal.
- Help with the washing up.
- Take the flowers home and the empty bottles away for recycling.
- Enjoy yourselves.

We certainly did! The food was beautifully cooked and served from a buffet by the caterers. The whole meal happened just like a well-planned military operation!

The menu was as follows:

- Gazpacho accompanied by bread sticks.
- Chicken breast stuffed with apricots and herbs.
- Savoury rice.
- Tossed green salad.
- Strawberry Pavlova.
- Rich chocolate torte.
- Tea and coffee.

Generous amounts of wine, beer, fruit juices and mineral water were available throughout the celebration.

Cake and Speeches:

When the tables had been cleared and the washing up complete the yard bell sounded yet again for the countdown to cake cutting.

In the heady fragrance of a summer's evening, guests gathered to drink the health of Chrissy and Vox. Vox made a short speech in which he thanked everyone for coming to help celebrate their special day.

The three-tier cake had been made by a friend and was decorated with tiny models of the symbol that had brought them together, two Smart cars, one red and one green.

A commemorative book was passed amongst the guests to be signed.

Entertainment:

Dusk was falling as everybody returned to the main barn. Musicians re-assembled, this time really letting their hair down as they combined their skills as a jazz band. The bride, still wearing her wedding dress, took her place in the band with her saxophone as they started by playing a waltz, 'I'll be Loving you Always' which was followed with such favourites as 'I Love Suzie.' Several times during the evening Chrissie left the band to snatch a dance with Vox. Music and dancing continued until late.

Departure:

Following breakfast next morning, taken with fellow campers, Chrissy and Vox left, each driving their own Smart car. Both vehicles were covered with balloons that had to be removed before they could be driven safely.

Gifts:

Instead of gifts Vox and Chrissie asked for donations to be made to a charity that they both supported.

Notes:

Chrissy and Vox were married at the register office a week or so after their party, having previously given notice of their intention and completed the legal formalities.

NORTH COMES SOUTH

A civil marriage ceremony and reception for twenty-five guests was followed by a celebratory cricket match with tea for one hundred that took place a week later.

Transporting a group of elderly folk south or a large party north was the dilemma for Lucy and Dave. After our discussion the following solution unfolded.

Action Plan:
Dave and Lucy grew up in the north of England before moving south to follow their chosen careers. Both sets of parents were elderly and not in the best of health, hence travelling was difficult for them. The couple decided to get married in Lucy's home town with their families and a few old friends in attendance. Their new friends, colleagues and the cricket team of which Dave was a keen member would celebrate in the south the following weekend with a cricket match and sumptuous tea.

A visit home prior to the wedding included seeing the Registrar who requested them to obtain a Notice of Intention to Marry from the register office in the area in which they lived. Having obtained the necessary legal documentation the ceremony could be held in a register office that was convenient for their parents. The couple were encouraged to choose their own readings and music providing they were non-religious. A plentiful choice of CDs was available from the register office library. It was with relief they discovered that the marriage room and adjacent waiting room were on the ground floor with easy wheelchair access. A loop system had been installed to assist the hard of hearing.

Invitations:
Twenty-five places at the register office governed the size of the wedding party. Immediate family mem-

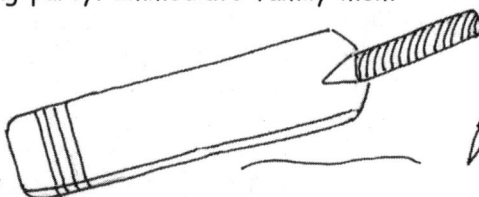

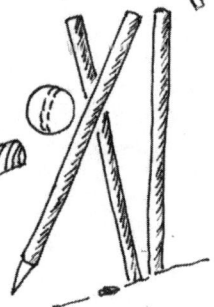

bers and a few long standing friends were invited to the ceremony and afterwards to the reception.

Bridal Wear:
Rather conscious of her hips Lucy chose a flattering dress with a long jacket in pale blue silk. The wide brim of her hat was softened with feathers in a contrasting shade of blue and she carried a hand-tied posy of white freesia and tight pink rosebuds.

Lucy observed an old tradition for her wedding. She wore something old, something new, something borrowed and something blue with a silver sixpence in her shoe. Her hat was borrowed, her suit was blue, she wore an antique silver bracelet left to her by an aunt and her shoes were new into which she slipped the silver sixpence. Although this was uncomfortable the tradition represented wealth, good luck and happiness.

Groom's Wear:
Dave and Garry, his best man, both wore lounge suits with pink rose buds in their buttonholes.

Photography:
The couple decided against having an official photographer, as among the guests were a number of enthusiastic amateurs who they knew would do an excellent job.

Marriage Ceremony:
Furnished in shades of burgundy and pink, the marriage room was light, airy and comfortable. The wedding party assembled as the voice of Celine Dion on CD sang 'My Heart Will go On', a song special to the bridal pair. The Superintendent Registrar introduced himself and his colleague, welcoming everybody to the marriage of Lucy and Dave. He requested that flash photography should not take place during the actual signing of the register and mobile telephones be switched off. Family and friends witnessed the joining in marriage of Lucy Anne and David James. The couple exchanged rings, which represented a visible seal to their marriage and following their embrace they were declared husband and wife. Having signed the register the Registrar presented Lucy with the marriage certificate and the party made their exit to Whitney Houston's hit 'I will Always Love You'.

The Setting:
A hotel with easy access, just a comfortable stroll from the register office was booked for the reception. The original oak beams, inglenook fireplace, fresh flowers in highly polished copper pots and the friendly staff offered a warm welcome.

Drinks:
Guests chose their favourite tipple from the bar; Dave had previously set money aside with the barman to cover the bar tariff.

Refreshments:
Guests moved through to the private dining room where the meal was to be served. Tables forming a horseshoe were clothed in pale pink linen with a single rosebud placed on each napkin marking the place setting. Lucy and Dave had previously chosen a three-course package that included wine and champagne.

The menu was as follows:

- Carrot and coriander soup served with rolls and butter.
- Noisette of lamb with red currant jelly, mint sauce and roast potatoes.
- Aubergine and tomato crumble for the vegetarians.
- A selection of fresh vegetables.
- Baileys and white chocolate crème brûlée.

The meal ended with filter coffee and champagne truffles.

Cake and Speeches:
Glasses of pink champagne were circulated in readiness for the speeches, which it was agreed would be short. Dave's nerves overtook him. He wanted the formalities to be over quickly. From a few scribbled notes he thanked everyone for coming and for the wedding presents he and Lucy had received.

In his speech Garry cracked several jokes around Dave's passion for cricket. It was a surprise to all when a cake was carried in, secretly ordered by Garry, made to represent a cricket pitch that even included tiny players. This linked the theme with the cricket match that was to take place the following week. Garry also used the occasion to present his gift of a silver cake knife to Lucy and Dave. Traditionally, on accepting a knife as a gift, coins must be exchanged in order not to cut a friendship.

The newlyweds eventually left in a shower of confetti, returning to their hotel for a while. During the evening they met with their families for refreshments and to open wedding presents.

Before travelling south next day they treated their parents to Sunday lunch, presenting both mums with an enormous bouquet of flowers and the dads with a bottle of their favourite tipple to say thank you.

The Cricket Match

The next weekend Dave and Lucy celebrated their marriage with a cricket match, followed by tea for one hundred.

Invitations:
Invitations had been sent requesting that friends form two teams for a friendly cricket match that would be followed by tea to include players' families. Mention was made that special entertainment and treats would be provided for the children.

An enclosed note read: 'Please do not bring presents but help us create a time capsule. Bring articles that will not deteriorate, no larger than a box of cooks' matches. Choose items that are symbolic of the day, date or occasion. Please mark them with your family name. They will be ceremoniously sealed into a container during the afternoon. All being well the capsule will be opened on our twenty-fifth wedding anniversary'.

Dress:
Dave wore his whites and a cap embroidered with the word 'Groom'.
Lucy wore her 'Bride' cap with jeans and a sweater.

The Setting:
Everyone assembled on the village green for the cricket match, overlooked by many individual and beautiful old, thatched cottages, the church and the Six Crowns Public House.

There was an enclosed play area nearby with swings, a slide, sea-saws and roundabouts for the younger children and space for ball games. A bouncy castle was also provided together with a Punch and Judy show that took place during the afternoon.

Dave borrowed a scout tent in exchange for a small donation that created an extension to the cricket pavilion just in case it rained.

Refreshments:
Plenty of cold beers, soft drinks, and cups of tea were provided, together with an old-fashioned tea of hearty sandwiches, scones and home-made cakes. There was great excitement when the ice cream van arrived at a pre-arranged time with many mouth-watering choices.

Entertainment:
Contributions to the time capsule were assembled and packed into a large tin and the lid ceremoniously sealed with sticky tape and sealing wax.

Among the contents were:

- Collection of current postage stamps.

- Newspaper cuttings relevant to the day.
- Lucky charms.
- Set of currency.
- Mobile phone.
- Jewellery.
- Everyday objects.
- Words of wisdom.
- Jokes and more.

Gifts:
A cricket bat signed by Dave's team was presented to the newlyweds with a special message of congratulations.

SOUL MATES

*A hand-fasting ceremony with a Celtic flavour and agape
(love feast) took place on the beach for forty guests,
followed by a quiet civil ceremony at a later date.*

While staying with a friend I offered to help co-ordinate and arrange the food and drinks for this wedding. To take part in such an
unusual celebration was for me a thoroughly enjoyable experience.

Action Plan:
American-born Brad was nearing the end of his stay in England when
he and Laura met by chance, or was it? As the morning mist was lifting
to reveal breathtaking views of the rugged coastline Laura was capturing
the scene with her watercolours and Brad had the same idea but with his
camera. It was love at first sight and a whirlwind romance followed.

The couple made an appointment with the registrar to enquire about arranging a civil marriage. They were advised that a civil ceremony could
not take place in less than sixteen days. Brad also checked his position
and discovered that as a representative of the UN he needed only the
standard documents. He arranged to stay with Laura for seven days
to fulfil his required time of residency. On the eighth day they
returned to the register office to complete the legal paperwork,
which had to be displayed on the public notice-board for fifteen
days. The wedding could then take place on the sixteenth day. Due
to their tight time schedule they arranged to hold a spiritual ceremony and party that would precede their civil marriage.

Invitations:
The invitations were crafted using copies of the watercolour that
Laura had been painting when she and Brad met. A sketched map was
provided indicating the car park and cove at which the celebration
would take place. Guests were asked not to bring gifts but it was
suggested that contributions towards the vegetarian meal would be
appreciated.

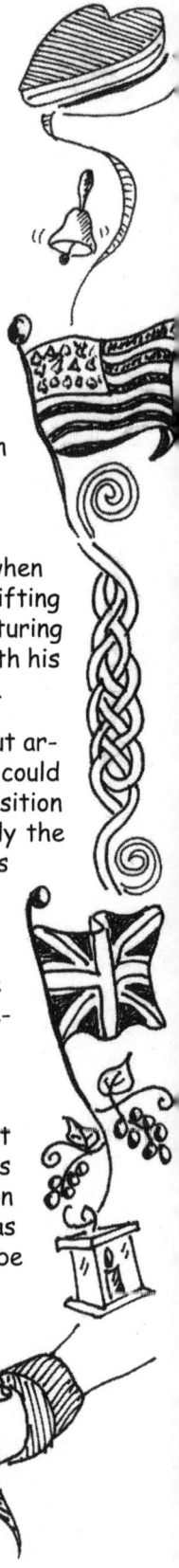

Hen and Stag Parties:
Laura's sister Sally organised the hen night. She invited a group of friends to supper and asked them to each bring a small item of significance that reminded them of Laura. As each treasure was placed in an ornate box, the memories and connections were explained. Laura was given the filled box as a gift.

Brad enjoyed a deep sea fishing trip with a few friends, which ended with a barbecue on the beach.

Bride and Groom's Wear:
Bare footed, Brad and Laura wore similar outfits in white organic cotton of simple design. On her head Laura wore a circlet of fresh herbs and carried a matching posy of rosemary, thyme and chamomile. Around their necks they both wore Celtic crosses. These were their wedding gifts to one another.

Attendants:
Each attendant represented one of the four elements:

- A girl in a flame coloured dress carried a lantern that symbolised 'fire'.
- A boy in a brown tunic and leggings carried a bowl of sand that represented 'earth'.
- A girl in a long pastel blue robe carried a jug of water.
- A boy in a silver tunic carried a small bell that he rang to symbolise 'air'.

Photography:
Friend Jon took a collection of un-posed black and white photographs throughout the celebration, adding hand-coloured details to some of the shots at a later date.

Hand-fasting Ceremony:
The procession led by a drummer could be heard approaching. Laura and Brad followed hand in hand with an arch of greenery held high above their heads by two girls. The four elements followed, guiding the guests along the beach towards the chosen cove where the rugged cliffs formed a backdrop of natural beauty for the gathering. A large circle indicating the circle of life had been etched in the sand, marking the spot where the ceremony was to take place. The fire in the centre was already burning with driftwood as the party approached.

With the archway of greenery now forming an entrance to the circle the bride and groom passed beneath to be welcomed by Sally who was to officiate at the ceremony. The four elements took their places at compass points around the circle followed by the guests. A Celtic blessing was offered with thanks to the elements as the couple acknowledged each one in turn.

Brad and Laura made their vows and exchanged rings, each with an intricately woven Celtic knot design. Sally began by explaining that a handfasting is a formal agreement between two people and that once the knot is tied woe betide anybody who undoes it!

She bound Laura and Brad's hands together loosely with coloured ribbons that reinforced the blessings of the elements and the couple promised to reaffirm their commitment to one another annually. Friends in turn contributed a selection of inspirational readings and poetry to the ceremony.

The agape, consisting of bread, grapes and wine, began when Sally broke bread from a loaf and offered a piece to the newly bonded couple saying: "May the love of the spirit be with you".

Laura and Brad fed each other with the pieces, then passed the loaf on to the guests who in turn broke off a fragment. This ritual was repeated by handing around the grapes and finally a goblet of wine.

Brad and Laura embraced then held the evergreen archway, this time allowing guests to pass beneath. A passage of clasped hands was formed through which Laura and Brad walked. Blessings, congratulations and hugs were exchanged.

Drinks:
Anchored by tin cans full of pebbles a tented canopy had been erected on the beach to provide shelter, either from rain or sunshine. Beers and organic country wines were served with plenty of non-alcoholic choices and bottled mineral water that were chilled in a fishing net placed where the incoming tide washed over them. A single guitarist strolled among the guests strumming gently at the strings and singing.

Refreshments:
Contributions of food were attractively arranged on a large cloth spread on the rocks and decorated with seashells and pebbles. Even meat eaters consumed the wide range of vegetarian dishes with relish.

Cake and Speeches:
The bride and groom cut a heart-shaped honey cake that had been made, iced and decorated by a friend as a gift. They fed one other with the first slice and drank mead from goblets that had been engraved with their entwined initials. Before friend David read some romantic poetry he asked everyone to drink a toast to Laura and Brad.

Entertainment:
Guests danced in circles, lines and spirals to the beat of the drum and sang to the strumming guitar or just sat by the fire talking.

Departure:

As dusk was falling the couple prepared to leave. Hand in hand they jumped over the dying embers of the fire, thereby following an old fertility rite. Everyone joined hands, forming a tight coil of bodies, which developed into a 'group hug'. Finally guests were given lighted flares to illuminate the way to where a small speed-boat was anchored.

After helping Laura aboard Brad pulled the starter and as the engine sprang to life they sped into the moonlight. Looking back only the lighted flares against the night sky could be seen.

Civil Ceremony:

With two legally required witnesses present Laura and Brad were married during a civil ceremony the following week. Laura chose to retain her own surname.

Gifts:

Brad and Laura had a star named after them. This original gift included a book, a picture and CD.
Website: www.starlistings.co.uk

Brad's family continued an American tradition by giving the couple a hand-made, appliquéd, wedding quilt that had been signed with loving messages.

Notes:

Before finalising the wedding arrangements, Brad checked the tidal time-tables. He also notified the coastguard that flares would be lit at dusk.

Permission to hold a private gathering on the beach had been obtained from the local council.

Laura, being environmentally aware, was somewhat embarrassed when she realised that Brad had changed their idea of leaving by rowing boat to a speed-boat but he decided that this would create a far more dramatic ending to their day.

CARIBBEAN CARNIVAL

A post honeymoon party for one hundred and fifty guests followed an intimate wedding in the Caribbean.

Creating salads from exotic ingredients, making litres of delicious coconut ice cream, rum punch tastings, the aroma of roasting hog and simply being part of this wonderful occasion made an extremely enjoyable day's work. Clearing up the next morning wasn't nearly such fun!

Action Plan:
Lawrence and Julie dreamed of a romantic wedding. After much contemplation they decided on a Caribbean package.

Their first step, as legally required, was to make an appointment at the register office in the districts in which they lived, in order to give notice of their intention to marry. To be married in the Caribbean they required a Certificate of No Impediment. The travel company checked all legal formalities and relevant documents. The quoted price included the flight, hotel accommodation, wedding ceremony and reception, cake, flowers, and photography. Close family members were able to travel with the couple at discounted rates.

The wedding party enjoyed a sunset cruise the night before the ceremony. Standing on deck they sipped glasses of chilled champagne as they gazed across the ocean at the moonlight spilling over the Caribbean sea.

Next day Julie and Lawrence married in accordance with local law. Making their vows and exchanging rings in a civil ceremony on a sun-drenched beach, surrounded by their nearest and dearest. Following the reception the newly married couple departed for their honeymoon retreat, where they enjoyed plenty of peaceful relaxation, scuba diving and snorkelling off the sandy shores.

Marrying overseas meant that only a few people were able to attend the wedding but a party was organised for their return that would include all their friends.

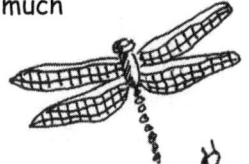

For the occasion Julie booked the hall, pool, cloakrooms and catering facilities at the school where she taught. These facilities were available for public hire in the holidays.

Invitations:
One hundred and fifty guests received party invitations decorated with palm trees and blue ocean requesting that they come dressed for the Caribbean and bring swimsuits.

Lawrence and Julie were unsure whether to include a wedding gift list but eventually decided that it would save a lot of time and hassle for everybody if they did. They chose a popular store where they were provided with hand-held scanners. As they made their way around each department they pointed the scanner at the barcode on their chosen items before returning to the Gift List Suite. Here their choices were downloaded on to computer. If they wished to make changes later they could do so online from home.

Bridal Wear:
The dress in which Julie had been married showed off her wonderful tan. It was a simple floor-length strapless gown of moonlight silk with a knot-ted back detail. She wore this for the party with a camellia in her hair.

Groom's Wear:
Lawrence wore a white linen suit and a bow tie, which had also been his wedding day attire.

Photography:
The album containing the couple's wedding photographs was on display for guests to browse through. Table cameras were distributed, in the hope of capturing many fun moments during the evening.

The Setting:
In their art classes Julie's students had been delighted with the challenge of transforming the austere surroundings of the school hall into a tropical island paradise. Brightly coloured tissue-paper flowers and palm trees were made and a beach scene backdrop painted for the bar. Well-anchored shiny helium balloons added a colourful Caribbean touch to the surroundings in which toucans, parrots, dragonflies and exotic flowers flourished.

Shallow bowls of floating candles and flower heads decorated the occasional tables.

Drinks:
Laurence had ordered the drinks on a sale or return basis, ensuring that

stocks would not run out. The arrangement included the glasses and allowed for any unopened and undamaged bottles to be returned.

Made from an original Caribbean recipe the rum punch consisted of 'one measure of sour, two sweet, three strong and four weak'.

For safety around the pool drinks were served in plastic glasses, but not ordinary ones, these flashed and created a magical effect in the twilight.

Refreshments:
After a few wicked rum punches, guests began to relax, dancing to the rhythmical beat of the steel band.

From a spit rose the delicious aroma of roasting hog that was later carved and served with plenty of crackling, savoury stuffing and apple sauce. A rowing boat decorated with fishing nets, pebbles and shells acted as an unusual buffet table, on which a wide selection of salads were displayed.

Dessert was a gigantic fruit salad made from a combination of tropical fruits that included pineapple, papaya, lychee and mango, served with lashings of coconut ice cream.

Cake and Speeches:
Lawrence and Julie met while learning to scuba-dive. Their two-tier wedding cake was therefore decorated to depict an underwater scene with a pair of dancing dolphins on the top tier. Julie's colleague made the rich black cake following a traditional Caribbean recipe. The succulent pineapple and dried fruits had been marinated in rum for days and the addition of coconut transformed it into a tropical delight.

In his speech, Lawrence remembered that with such a gathering of friends he had a lot going for him. He established common ground with everyone as soon as he got to his feet by referring to the good food and music in glowing terms. He proceeded to recall his first date with Julie and included several amusing and exaggerated tales about their underwater exploration. The stories that he told were all chosen for their humorous content and they didn't fail. He knew their friends were usually easy to please and ready to laugh at just about anything, and they did.

Entertainment:
The atmosphere was electric as bodies gyrated to the pulsating sounds of calypso music, guests danced the samba, cha-cha-cha, bossa nova, bolero and plenty of pop.

While the band had a break, a limbo dancing display took place that was followed by an opportunity to have a go! Those who needed to 'cool off' enjoyed a dip in the pool.

Departure:
On leaving, everyone was impressed by the fairy lights strung in the trees that lined the long driveway.

I agreed with Julie and Lawrence that the doors be firmly closed until our return in the morning to clear up.

Gifts:
The opportunity to swim with dolphins was a much appreciated gift to the couple.

Notes:
Lawrence obtained helpful advice and tips for speech-making at a private session with Robert Alan Haven who lectures on public speaking and is an after dinner speaker.
E-mail: robertalanhaven@onetel.com

Flashing battery operated plastic glasses are available from UK Art Group Ltd.
Website: www.glowunlimited.com

CYBERSPACE

A virtual wedding experience, followed by a civil marriage ceremony and a reception for seventy-five guests in a gallery of modern art and crafts.

Alice's parents had hoped to give their only daughter a traditional wedding but Bjorn and Alice had little connection with the church. When their engagement was made public a compromise was reached. They planned a civil marriage that would be followed by a reception to honour Bjorn's Swedish ancestry that was a little different.

Action Plan:
Alice and Bjorn met on the internet in a chat room, which led to a great deal of time being spent online getting to know one another. Alice eventually revealed to Bjorn that she had been deaf since birth. This resulted in her having difficulty with speech although her lip-reading was good. Bjorn was amazed at this revelation as he was also deaf having himself contracted childhood meningitis. Fortunately he had retained his speech. This shared knowledge bonded the couple and they decided just for fun to experience a cyberspace marriage online. It felt comfortable and safe since no speech was necessary. They cherished their virtual certificates of marriage even though they were not legally binding. A few weeks later Bjorn and Alice met face to face for the first time.

Proposal:
While on a picnic Bjorn proposed to Alice after producing a bottle of chilled champagne, two glasses and an engagement ring. Alice e-mailed her family and cyber friends, giving them the exciting news.

Bjorn and Alice attended an appointment at the register office in their districts of residence to give notice of their intention to marry. Sweden being inside the EEA meant that Bjorn did not require any additional docu-

mentation. They also checked the availability of a loop system in the office to help the hard of hearing and mentioned that a signer would be present on the day.

Invitations:
The wedding invitations were designed to be as individual as the couple. Each guest received a personalised card containing a CD that not only contained the invitation to the big day but also told the story in print and sound of Bjorn and Alice's relationship from how they first met to the proposal. Guests were asked to pledge gifts of money that could be spent in the gallery of modern art where the reception was to take place, as the couple were keen to purchase several larger items. Directions and details of local accommodation were also included on the CD.

Hen and Stag Parties
Rather than have separate parties, the couple decided to celebrate together. Having searched the internet for ideas, it was Bjorn's vision of heaven to spend a few days in Brussels that included a tour of a chocolate factory, hopefully leading to lots of free samples.

Bridal Wear:
Alice chose an elegant bias-cut dress in purple on which she wore a corsage of silk flowers in toning shades of pink and mauve, this left her hands free to use sign language, also solving the problem of her allergy to pollen. She followed the tradition of many Swedish brides by placing a silver coin from her father in her left shoe and a gold coin from her mother in her right shoe, meaning that she will never do without!

Groom's Wear:
Bjorn wore dark trousers, a cream open-neck shirt and purple velvet waistcoat. His brother who was best man dressed in a similar style.

Civil Ceremony:
During the civil ceremony attended by immediate family members Alice and Bjorn made their vows and exchanged rings that consisted of three twisted bands of white gold symbolising betrothal, marriage and parenthood. They hired the services of a registered signer who interpreted the proceedings from speech to sign and sign to speech.

Photography:
Using a digital camera, photographs were taken by a friend who was a keen amateur photographer, both at the civil ceremony and reception. At a later date Bjorn and Alice organised their own wedding website, which enabled everyone to share treasured memories and post their own personal greetings on-line.

Drinks:
After an intimate family lunch, everyone gathered for the reception at the gallery of modern art and crafts, where cocktails of champagne and peach schnapps were served and soft background music played on CD.

The photographer, looking down from a balcony, attracted the attention of the crowd by a camera flash and was rewarded by everyone looking up and raising their glasses. This was an original and informal way of capturing the entire wedding group.

The Setting:
The gallery of modern arts and crafts was originally opened to encourage young artists and crafts-people to exhibit and sell their work. Attractive items of furniture, glass, pottery, embroidery and paintings were among the work on display in the spacious, well-lit surroundings and many of the exhibits on show could be commissioned or purchased.

Pedestal arrangements of white silk flowers with fresh foliage combined with green grapes, apples and halved kiwi fruits were placed in the entrance hall. Strong colour was kept to a minimum thus avoiding any conflict with the works of art.

Refreshments:
Small circular tables and chairs provided informal seating for the meal. Guests were invited to take a plate (with a glass clip attached) and help themselves from the traditional Swedish smorgasbord that offered a wide range of delicacies. The open sandwich toppings included gravadlax with soured cream, prawns, pickled herrings, cheeses, cold meats, pickled cabbage and other specialities, all attractively arranged on crackers, pumpernickel and Scandinavian breads.

Knives and forks, rolled in a purple serviette and tied with matching ribbon, were placed beside glasses of red and white wine and beer awaiting collection at the end of the buffet.

Decorating the buffet was a vase of silver painted twigs with ribbons from which hung heart shaped ginger biscuits iced with the couple's initials.

Cake and Speeches:
To satisfy Bjorn's particular weakness, the wedding cake was a richly coated chocolate confection, decorated with a cascade of individual chocolates, which offered the perfect accompaniment to coffee. Bjorn gave his speech with the aid of a PowerPoint presentation, which helped him and also gave his guests something to look at. The best man's speech was in limerick and was delivered simultaneously in speech and sign language. He then handed the couple a beautifully framed copy as a keepsake. Many of the guests, also deaf, were able to add their own

interjections in sign language during the speeches, which all added to the fun.

Departure:
Bjorn carried his new wife to the two-seater red racing Bentley that awaited them. Helium filled latex balloons printed with the couple's names were released by guests as the car drove away.

Gifts:
Bjorn and Alice were invited to select presents from the many individual works of art on display in the gallery. Gifts of money were also pledged to pay for larger items that enabled them to commission several pieces of furniture.

Notes:
Bjorn and Alice searched the internet for ideas while planning their wedding.
Website: www.confetti.co.uk/weddings/advice

Restrictions within the gallery included a 'no smoking' rule and 'no live music'.

A virtual bulletin board was organised where friends could post notices to the couple free of charge. Alice and Bjorn sent their thanks via the same medium.

CIRCLES OF LIFE

A civil marriage and reception took place in Tenerife, followed in England by a service of blessing and a country garden reception for eighty guests. A fortieth birthday picnic took place a week later.

As you may have read in the introduction of *Your Day, Your Way*, Jenny and I met in the sixties, at the school gates, while collecting our children. A catering business eventually evolved from our homes in the small village in which we lived. It feels fitting to end this book with the most recent wedding that I have been involved with.

Of Jenny and Dave's five children Nicki was their only daughter, so when she and Carlos announced their intention to marry, there was a great excitement. Jenny put into action her skills as an expert cake maker and decorator, caterer and florist. It was a pleasure to help co-ordinate the incredible spread that she prepared using experience gained in a lifetime of organised preparation.

Action Plan:
Living happily in Tenerife with their nine-year-old son, Joshua, Nicki and Spanish-born Carlos eventually decided to tie the knot. Plans for their English country garden reception began to evolve with a pink, white and silver theme, which was reflected throughout the arrangements. A date was chosen just prior to Nicki's fortieth birthday so that their wedding in Tenerife was followed by three special occasions crammed into a few weeks on intense partying, surprises and emotion.

Civil Ceremony:
Both large families witnessed Nicki and Carlos's civil marriage ceremony in Tenerife. Following the formalities the party drove to a restaurant high in the hills with magnificent views where they tucked into a feast of local fare and danced to a salsa band.

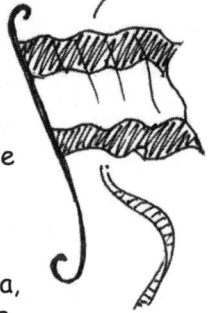

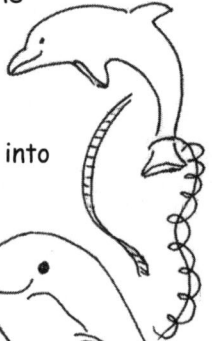

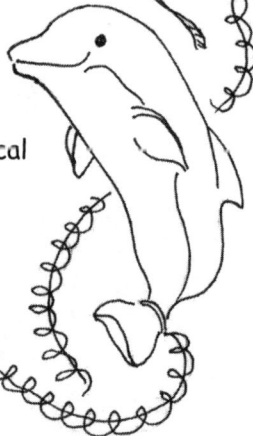

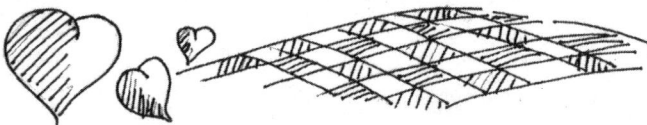

Later that week the newlyweds travelled to England with their son and all seventeen members of the English side of the family on the same flight.

Invitations:
One glance at the invitations gave promise of a treat to come. A photograph of sweet peas in gentle pastel shades, matching ribbon and two sparkly pink love hearts invited guests to the blessing ceremony of Nicola Clare and Juan Carlos Martin.

Bridal Wear:
For both the marriage and blessing Nicki wore a simple dress of white linen, which flattered her well-tanned skin and blue eyes. Her fair hair was styled into ringlets with tiny sprigs of white gypsophila tucked amongst the curls. Made by her mother in the early hours of the morning her bouquet was fresh, fragrant and fragile, consisting of roses, lilies and sweet peas in white and gentle shades of pink and lavender.

Groom's Wear:
Both Carlos and his best man Michael, one of Nicki's brothers, wore dark suits with white shirts, silver ties and white rosebuds in their buttonholes.

Attendants:
Nicki's three small nieces were bridesmaids. Their pale lilac organza dresses were also worn for the second time and they carried hand-tied bunches of delicately coloured sweet peas with trailing pink ribbons.

Joshua and his cousin were pageboys and wore silver waistcoats with dark trousers and white shirts.

Photography:
Long-standing friends of Nicki, Fiona and her husband, both photographers flew from Australia using the wedding as an excuse for their own honeymoon. Over a thousand digital images were taken, which included shots of the family cats and many stolen romantic moments. There certainly was no shortage of colourful photographic backdrops within the unique cottage garden.

Service of Blessing:
The service of blessing was held in the 12th century church in the heart of the village where Nicki's parents now live. Flowers used to decorate the church were chosen for their colour, perfume and the fact that they had to be arranged at great speed. Sweet peas in shades of purple and pink with gypsophila and carefully colour co-ordinated lilies and roses were used in the large arrangements. Posies of sweet peas were attached to the pew ends, which not only looked beautiful but also perfumed the whole church with their fragrance.

The covers of the order of service sheets were hand worked in delicate cross-stitch by a friend and bore the names of the couple and the date of the wedding.

Joshua carried the wedding rings in a small silver box. During the ceremony he handed the rings to the minister to be sanctified. After prayers, hymns and readings the minister blessed the happy couple.

Drinks:
A row of galvanized watering cans placed along the edge of the driveway contained bunches of fresh garden flowers in pastel shades, tied with raffia. Guests mingled on the manicured lawns of the picturesque tile-hung cottage. In the garage, refrigerators were lined up and the bar set beneath an awning attached to the up-and-over doors. As guests arrived, the men of the family served champagne.

A selection of hot and cold cocktail savouries were passed around including smoked salmon and cream cheese roulades, devils and angels on horseback, asparagus rolls, ham and paté rolls and various dips.

Beneath the awning, a table was set providing finger food and soft drinks for the younger children.

The Setting:
To gain access to the rear garden where a marquee had been erected, guests passed beneath an archway cascading with sweet scented honeysuckle, clematis and roses. Pink, white and lavender busy lizzies were bursting from hanging baskets, troughs and window boxes, the seeds of which had been sown by Dave in the spring.

Refreshments:
Nicki chose the original dishes that we served all those years ago and have since become tried and tested family favourites. Carlos' family and guests from Tenerife were also considered with tapas being part of the buffet.

The spread was covered in fine white muslin until it was time to eat, keeping the buffet fresh and insect-free.

The Menu was as follows:

- Coronation chicken.
- Cold roast turkey decorated with sprigs of fresh herbs
- Honey baked ham on the bone.
- Glazed and decorated Scottish salmon.
- Platters of continental meats.
- Cashew nut roast.

167

- Tapas of stuffed peppers, anchovies and tomatoes with goats' cheese.
- Fresh asparagus.
- An array of imaginative salads.
- French bread and butter.
- Cheese board.

Strawberries and clotted Cornish cream were served with wickedly rich chocolate rum torte, meringues and fresh fruit kebabs. Coffee followed, accompanied by pink and white marshmallows and heart shaped peppermint creams on which Jenny had iced the couple's initials.

The bridesmaids walked among the guests with a basket of bonbonniers and gave one to each lady. These dainty gifts were made of pink net tied with fine matching ribbon and contained five sugared almonds symbolising health, wealth, happiness, fertility and good fortune.

Cake and Speeches:
The wedding cake represented many hours of love and dedication. Two tiers of rich fruitcake were decorated with handmade sugar sweet peas, roses in pastel shades and trailing ivy that followed through the wedding theme. Fingers of cake were cut and placed into éclair cases to be eaten with coffee later in the evening.

Dave gave a short speech in well-polished Spanish in which he asked that everybody raise their glasses to toast the future happiness of "Nicki and Carlos."

During Carlos' speech that he made in English he presented Dave and Jenny with a 'bird jacuzzi' for their garden.

Michael told the story of how the family spent a holiday in Tenerife going on a day trip to watch whales and dolphins play. Carlos was the boat's skipper. To cut a long story short, said Michael: "Here they are thirteen years later tying the knot!"

A pair of helium-filled dolphin balloons on long ribbons was presented to Carlos and Nicki, one silver and one pink.

Entertainment:
A barbecue was arranged for the evening when friends provided the music for dancing and Jade, a fourteen-year-old relative sang 'Colours of the Wind' from Disney's 'Pocahontas'.

Five days after the wedding a family picnic took place on the village green to celebrate Nicki's fortieth birthday. With seventeen immediate family members each gathering became a party. On this occasion, Nicki's friends from the gymnastic club where she had been a member as a teenager came along to surprise her and yet another beautiful cake was produced.

The cricket pavilion was available in case of rain but fortunately was not needed.

Gifts:
One gift to Nicki and Carlos was a framed poem especially written for them into which all aspects of their lives were woven.

HERE, THERE AND EVERYWHERE

Home is an island bathing in sun
Where exuberant dolphins play and have fun
Leaping like gymnasts with true zest for life
Where Carlos and Nicki became man and wife

Home is a place where hollyhocks grow
Tended by loved ones who want you to know
That a garden awaits you on your special day
Your corner of England when you are away

Home is a village where Morris Men call
And there stands the Church of Saints Peter and Paul
Whose blessing upon you will always ensure
That with love all around you can never be poor

Home is a picnic enjoyed in a glade
That won't last forever – but memories don't fade
It's the joining of spirits of people who care
For you and each other and trusting they're there

Home is where family and friends want to come
To share in the joy with you both and your son
So remember as a married life you now start
Home will be with you it's inside your heart.

By Sharon Miller

Notes:
'Here There and Everywhere,' was written by Sharon Miller 'The Verse Nurse'.
Tel: 01903 639100
E-mail: R.S.Miller@btinternet.com

Friends and neighbours in the village offered accommodation to guests travelling from afar.

It was a pleasure to help co-ordinate this occasion. Having such a talented mother and a supportive, green-fingered father was a sure recipe for success. Hundreds of hours of loving preparation were revealed on the day with not a leaf left unturned.

Now in retirement, Jenny and I look back with fond memories of our little helpers, now responsible men and women with families of their own.

At the end of the celebrations we remembered how on numerous occasions in the past adrenaline alone had kept us going, working until we dropped! A circle completed.

MEMORIES TO SAVOUR

You will undoubtedly be reminded of your wonderful wedding long after the day itself, often in bizarre ways; a stray piece of confetti turning up in a coat pocket or finding a lost champagne glass during the winter in a leafless hedge. However, memories need not be left to chance and these are some suggestions you may wish to consider.

- Have your bouquet preserved or photographed.
- Write thank you letters on note-paper bearing digital images of your wedding.
- Fill a special box with wedding memorabilia.
- Make a garland with items collected on the day, e.g. champagne corks, cake decorations, place names, favours, lucky charms, etc.
- Make a board of memories using fabrics, ribbons, pressed flowers, photographs, etc.
- Create and frame a collage of snapshots, an ideal way to use the not so perfect ones.
- Fill a scrap book; love letters, wedding invitation, order of service, menu, photographs, gift cards, letters, etc.

CONCLUSION

I trust that you have found more than a tin of bully beef within these pages to inspire you when creating your individual and special day. Once a theme has been chosen other decisions fall easily into place. It is not only the pleasure of attending a wedding with a difference but also the evident attention given to small details that leave lasting impressions.

I hope you havefound inspiration in using this book to create *YOUR DAY, YOUR WAY* – an occasion that is individual, romantic and one that reflects your shared values and future hopes.

MILESTONE MENTOR SERVICE

Now in retirement, using the experience of a lifetime I offer a service whereby using e-mail and telephone I can help plan the special occasions that celebrate the milestones of life.

For further information:
Jean Francis
Tel: 01403 273754
E-mail: milestone-celebrations@uwclub.net

Also available from the Milestone Series:

Time To Go - Inspiriational Funerals

APPENDIX ONE

WEDDING CHECKLIST

THEME	
DATE	
TIME	
LOCATION OF SERVICE	
CELEBRANT, PRIEST, MINISTER OR REGISTRAR	
DOCUMENTS REQUIRED	
ATTENDANTS/PARTICIPANTS	
GUEST LIST	
OUTFITS	
RINGS	
TRANSPORT	
PHOTOGRAPHER/VIDEO	
INVITATIONS	
SERVICE SHEETS	
FLOWERS	
MUSIC	
LOCATION OF RECEPTION	
CAKE	
DRINKS	
CATERING	
TABLE PLAN	
SPEECHES	
ENTERTAINMENT	
DEPARTURE	
HONEYMOON	
FOREIGN CURRENCY	
PASSPORT	

APPENDIX TWO

ANNIVERSARIES

	Ancient	Modern
1st	Paper	Clocks
2nd	Cotton	China
3rd	Leather	Crystal/Glass
4th	Silk Flowers	Appliances
5th	Wood	Silverware
6th	Iron	Wood
7th	Copper	Desk Sets
8th	Bronze	Linen/Lace
9th	Pottery	Leather
10th	Tin	Diamond Jewellery
11th	Steel	Fashion Jewellery
12th	Linen	Pearls
13th	Lace	Textiles
14th	Ivory	Gold Jewellery
15th	Crystal	Watches
20th	China	Platinum
25th	Silver	Silver
30th	Pearl	Diamond
35th	Coral	Jade
40th	Ruby	Ruby
45th	Sapphire	Sapphire
50th	Gold	Gold
55th	Emerald	Emerald
60th	Diamond	Diamond

APPENDIX THREE

RECOMMENDED READING

Alternative Weddings – by Jane Ross McDonald
Published by Thorson.

Alternative Weddings – by Kate Gordon
Published by Constable.

Ceremonies of the Heart – by Becky Butler
Published by Seal Press.

Joining Hands and Hearts – by Revd. Susanna Macomb
Published by Simon Schuster.

Non-Traditional Weddings – by Diane Ffitch
Published by Hodder & Stoughton.

The Little Giant Encyclopedia of Wedding Etiquette
by Wendy Toliver
Published by Sterling.

Mitch Murray's One Liners for Weddings and How to Use Them In Your
Speech – by Mitch Murray
Published by Foulsham.

Before I say "I Do." How to be Happily Married for Ever
by Elizabeth Martyn.
Published by Vermillion.

Weddings: Everything You Need to Know – by Karen Dolby
Published by Harper Collins.

A Modern Girl's Guide to Getting Hitched – by Sarah Ivens.
Published by Piatkus.

Your Wedding, Your Way – by Sophie Vincent
Published by Ebury Press.

Creating Ceremony – by Glennie Kindred and Lu Garner
Tel: 07990 553270 or 01335 370754

APPENDIX FOUR

SOME USEFUL ADDRESSES

Baptist Union of Great Britain, PO Box 44, Baptist House,
129 The Broadway, Didcot, Oxon. OX11 8RT
Tel: 01235 517700
E-mail: info@baptist.org.uk
Website: www.baptist.org.uk

British Buddhist Association, 11 Biddulph Road, London. W9 1JA
Tel: 020 7286 5575

British Humanist Association, 47 Theobald's Road, London. WC1X 8SP
Tel: 020 74300908
Website: www.humanism.org.uk

Choice Ceremonies, 107 Salisbury Road, Totton,
Southampton. SO40 3HZ
Tel: 023 8086 1256
E-mail: Lesley@choiceceremonies.co.uk
Website: www.choiceceremonies.co.uk

Marriage Care, Clitherow House, 1 Blythe Mews, Blythe Road,
London. W14 0NW
Tel: 020 7371 1341
E-mail: angela@marriagecare.org.uk
Website: www.marriagecare.org.uk

Gay and Lesbian Humanist Association, The Pink Triangle Trust,
34 Spring Lane, Kenilworth, Warwickshire. CV8 2HB
Tel: 01926 858450
Email: secretary@pinktriangle.org.uk
Website: www.galha.org.uk

Interfaith Seminary.
Tel: 0207 368 3325
E-mail: theinterfaithseminary@community.co.uk
Website: www.interfaithseminary.org.uk
Jewish Marriage Council, 23 Ravenshurst Ave, London. NW4 4EE
Tel: 020 8203 6311
E-mail: info@jmc-uk.org

Website: www.jmc-uk.org

Lesbian and Gay Christian Movement, Oxford House,
Derbyshire Street, London. E2 6HG
Tel: 020 7739 1249
E-mail: lgcm@lgcm.org.uk
Website: www.lgcm.org.uk

Methodist Church, Westminster Central Hall, Storey's Gate,
London. SW1H 9NH
Tel: 020 7222 8010
Website: www.w-c-h.co.uk

Quakers Religious Society of Friends, Friends House,
173-177 Euston Road, London. NW1 2BJ
Tel: 020 7387 3601
Website: www.quaker.org.uk

Gretna Registration Office, Central Avenue, Gretna,
Scotland. DG16 5AQ
Tel: 01461 337648
E-mail: gretnaonline@dumgal.gov.uk
Website: www.gretnaonline.net

The General Assembly of Unitarian and Free Christian Churches,
Essex Hall, 1-6 Essex Street, London. WC2R 3HY
Tel: 020 7240 2384
E-mail: ga@unitarian.org.uk
Website: www.unitarian.org.uk

United Reformed Church, 86 Tavistock Place, London. WC1H 9RT
Tel: 020 7916 2020

For local information on places of worship and religious organisations, see
Yellow Pages.